How to Have

the Wedding

of Your

Dreams

on the

Budget of

Your Choice

Affordable
WEDDINGS

BY LETA W. CLARK

ILLUSTRATIONS BY ROBERT CURET

A FIRESIDE BOOK
Published by Simon & Schuster Inc.
New York • London • Toronto • Sydney • Tokyo

Copyright © 1988 by Leta W. Clark
Illustrations copyright © 1988 by Simon & Schuster

A FIRESIDE BOOK
Published by Simon & Schuster Inc.
Simon & Schuster Building
Rockefeller Center
1230 Avenue of the Americas
New York, NY 10020
FIRESIDE and colophon are registered trademarks of Simon & Schuster Inc.

Designed by Barbara Marks Graphic Design
Manufactured in the United States of America

10   9   8   7   6   5   4   3

Library of Congress Cataloging in Publication Data
Clark, Leta W.
    Affordable weddings.

    "A Fireside book."
    1. Weddings—United States—Planning.   I. Title.
HQ745.C55   1988   395′.22   87-28612
ISBN 0-671-64056-9

Grateful acknowledgment is given to Alan S. Munn, food manager aboard the *S.S. Amerikanis*, and to Ken G.
Deutsch, Catering Manager, Fairmont Hotel, San Francisco, for permission to quote them and use their information
concerning food preparation and presentation in this book.

▲ ▲ ▲ ▲ ▲ ▲ ▲

To Cath and Greg,

whose wedding

made this

book possible,

and to Mills

and Caroline,

whose weddings

have yet

to be.

▼ ▼ ▼ ▼ ▼ ▼ ▼

▲▲▲▲▲▲▲

CONTENTS

▼▼▼▼▼▼▼

▲▲▲▲▲▲▲

THE
APPROACH

▼▼▼▼▼▼▼

1

THE APPROACH

T▼▼▼▼▼▼▼his book came into being because, not too long ago, we were right where you are today—trying to figure out how to put on a terrific wedding. My daughter Catherine was going to marry her gentleman, Gregory, so a wedding had to be planned, executed, paid for, and celebrated. Who knew how to do that?

The family gathered—not just the immediate family, but the extended family, vestigial remnant of the plummier days of the '70s. Back then group activities were not only the best but often the only activities one did. Our extended family, the Carlottis, offers a wide range of talent and expertise, much of it related to the arts and performing arts. If anybody could prepare a wedding, I figured, we could.

And as a writer with less than a marvelous memory, I kept notes on how we prepared the wedding. Lots of notes, which friends and relatives have borrowed, used, and passed on to their friends. Occasionally when the notes arrive home again we match them up with the photographs of our gala event, get teary reliving the beautiful parts, and laugh ourselves silly over the mishaps. The glow of successful teamwork infuses our memories, and we have little doubt that it was one of our collective finest hours. We didn't function like a well-oiled machine or a Marine drill team; we bumped along and made it happen our way, and you can do that, too.

▲▲▲▲▲▲▲

HOW WE DID IT

▽▽▽▽▽▽▽

Establishing the scope of the wedding was the first eye-opener. "Let's invite everybody! It can't be one of those meager affairs. Let's make it fantastic, with lots of attendants, music, flowers, great food. . . . Remember when Prince Charles married Lady Diana and we all watched on television? Let's do it like that."

As a senior Carlotti, I was one of the few who had ever attended, much less participated in, a true formal wedding. The barefoot-in-a-field-with-tambourines-clinking ceremony was much more familiar to everybody else and was not remotely what Cath and Greg wanted: life had changed. It was time to bring out the white gloves.

While I struggled to remember how people used to do it, Cath and Greg made up our guest list. The numbers were astounding but paled considerably when we got Greg's mother's list. Now that was a list! It resembled a small town's telephone directory. Noting our dismay, Greg said mildly, "Real Italians have big families. I guess you didn't know that. . . ."

We finally narrowed it down to 275 people, not counting children. A mistake. Children need seats at tables, food, and more soft drinks than you can imagine. Still, 275 gave us a number to work with, so we moved along into budget planning. We knew weddings were big money events, especially in the middle of New York City where everything seems to cost more than it should. But we needed a bottom line money estimate.

Unfortunately, in the same year as the wedding, Caroline, Catherine's younger sister, was going off to college, an expensive college in a pretty New England town. It didn't take much research to show us we had about two thousand dollars that could be earmarked for the grand event. Everything else was already allocated.

Greg's mother—that unknown "Other Mother"—was understandably upset when she got wind of the situation. In subsequent years I have played out in my head many conversations she may have had concerning our wedding budget. Whether any or all of these dialogues were true is irrelevant. A few days later she graciously slipped Greg a thousand dollars with no strings attached to help with the costs.

And, oddly enough, the three thousand dollars seemed like an acceptable figure for a 275-person wedding. I see now that the jump from two thousand to three thousand was what made it look good.

THE APPROACH

▲▲▲▲▲▲▲

HOW YOU CAN DO IT

▼▼▼▼▼▼▼

But enough about us. Let's talk about you. . . .

Let us assume you have some very definite ideas about your wedding, ideas that have led you to reject a mass-produced, catered affair. Probably you have shopped around a bit, read the bridal magazines, and are feeling rather glum.

Perhaps you are appalled at the exorbitant cost and the paucity of choices available to you in a mass-produced wedding. Maybe you are marrying again and want to create a very personal celebration the second time around. Or you have been living together for so long that the catered affair seems kind of silly when a terrific party is what you want.

Whatever the reasons, you've decided to do it your own way. Be assured: It can be done. Designing your own wedding allows you to follow the traditions in a way that reflects your own personal taste, and producing your own celebration gives you the flexibility to place your money exactly where you feel it will do the most for you.

Giving a wedding is similar to producing a show. The early weeks of organizing, budgeting, and staff meetings tumble together, racing toward the dress rehearsal, the last-minute revisions, and then— opening night. The music sounds, the bridesmaids start down the aisle, and the show begins.

Nobody produces a show, be it wedding or Shakespeare, without money. You know

you will need to budget money for items such as:

Space
Invitations
Clothing
Food and beverages
Flowers and decorations
Sound and music
Lighting
Photography
Clergy or official

A quick examination of the cost estimates from a catering place or a wedding consultant indicates the major expense in most of these categories is the labor cost. Nicely enough, labor is what you and most couples have access to—volunteer labor from glowing relatives and enthusiastic friends.

Chances are, all you have to do is ask. Most of us are pleased to be asked to lend a hand, especially if the request is in an area in which we take pride. It lets us know our special achievements are recognized, be they arranging flowers, taking sensitive photographs, or tending bar with a hospitable hand. The gift of assistance is often far more important and enduring than the set of matching towels sent from the local department store.

Say, for example, your mother's best friend makes the most wonderful chicken salad you've ever tasted. That best friend is a logical candidate for the wedding reception food category. Or say your cousin is a whiz at stereos and sound systems. That cousin can be approached about setting up the music and sound system for the reception.

There are also the young friends and relatives who think your wedding is the most exciting event they've ever come across. They might not have developed areas of expertise yet, but their energy and enthusiasm can be joyously applied to many "real" tasks. Pre-wedding jobs may include unpacking and keeping a log of presents; addressing, stamping, and mailing announcements and invitations; measuring and cataloging tables, chairs, and furnishings that will be used for the reception; and other portions of the event.

The ceremony and the reception offer great possibilities for teens and young people. They can act as official doormen, car dispatchers, candle lighters, bus and bar boys, coat checkers, and food servers; they can identify guests for the photographer, cue the musicians, and be in charge of the newlyweds' going-away outfits and luggage. (Note that I'm not even mentioning the ceremonial decorating of the going-away car. I'll leave that to their imagination!)

This book can help you turn a group of happy volunteers into a competent, efficient staff. Each chapter explores an area of your wedding, from flowers to sound systems, that you will need to consider. Solid how-to advice from professionals will help demystify the wedding process and bring it back to what it was for centuries: a lovely folk celebration honoring the deepest commitment two people can make.

You may choose to do the entire production yourselves, or you may select portions and hire professionals to do the rest. Generally, a wedding consultant is an expert in all areas and can be em-ployed in many capacities, from doing the entire event to taking over a single category. A party planner or caterer can create the reception you want, often working with the florist either of you chooses. Personal shoppers are available if shopping makes you crazy; bridal shops or bridal sections in department stores can take over the work of outfitting everyone.

Musicians, DJs, printers, calligraphers, photographers, social secretaries, and more, are out there if you need them. Just check your local classified telephone directory. The costs will vary in different locales, but be aware that you can always hire pros to do anything you feel you don't want to tackle yourselves.

If you decide to employ outside help, read through the appropriate chapters before your first meeting so you can have a list of questions ready. Comparison shop, of course, and always check at least two or, better yet, three recent references before you make a final decision. "Recent" is the key word here; people and staffs change, and not always for the better.

▲▲▲▲▲▲▲

IT'S ALL BASED ON A MASTER PLAN, WORKSHEETS, AND SHEER DELIGHT

▼▼▼▼▼▼▼

Keep in mind that producing a sizable wedding is a massive amount of work and

T H E   A P P R O A C H

requires a lot of time. Ask yourselves where the extra hours can come from in everyone's busy schedules. This book will help you plan and organize the celebration, making the most efficient use of the volunteers you recruit. Be sure everybody who wants to help understands fully the amount of time involved, so the commitments can be honored.

Andrea Randall, Manager in Charge of Scenic Services for NBC's Burbank Studios, says, "Any production, no matter how complicated, has to be divided into categories. The categories are then broken down into work units, and a chain of command is developed for each unit. Once the structure is established, the workers can be brought in."

Andrea's point is well taken. Every production must be pulled apart and reorganized into tasks that people can actually handle. Volunteers become productive workers when they know exactly what is required of them and for what length of time. It illustrates your respect for their talents—not to be taken lightly—and frees them to enjoy the rest of the party when their job is done.

Borrowing from the stage manager's bag of tricks, we have divided the overall wedding activity into smaller, more manageable categories. Within each area we have worked out a series of assignable tasks that can then be matched up to the potential volunteers list.

The worksheets at the back of this book will help you organize your volunteers, resources, and budget. In many cases you will want to remove the worksheets, have them photocopied, and distribute them so all your volunteers have the identical in-

formation about their responsibilities. Or you can post the worksheets of the food and beverage service areas at the wedding itself as on-location checklists.

To carry the theatrical analogy a bit further, begin as though you are the producers and visualize the wedding as an event that will delight you and your audience. *Eliminate all preconceptions.* You are putting on a show starring you—the couple of the year! Try to view the entire span of festivities, from engagement through reception, as one continuous, traveling celebration of a very important event.

You know what best delights you, so build it in! You know what circumstances will make you sparkle, so make sure you'll have lots of opportunities to shine. Edit out anything dreary and plan to include the things you enjoy. You like candlelight? Great—use it. Like fireworks? Prince Charles and Lady Di certainly delighted the world with their prenuptial fireworks display. If they're legal in your state, get some!

Producers begin with a concept, focusing on the overall feeling and message they want their production to convey. Spend an evening or two conceptualizing your show. Are you favoring an old-fashioned lace-and-roses wedding? Are you happier with an up-to-the-minute, trendy celebration? What's best for you?

Take it further into the visuals and begin to "see" the ceremony as if you are watching it on television. A wedding is one of the best pageants in the world. Imagine the processional as you, your friends and family walk down the aisle. How does everybody look? How does the music sound? What kind of lighting is there? How do the flowers smell?

Use the worksheet on page 190 to help inspire and organize your vision.

Producers often use "storyboards" to conceptualize a production, be it a commercial or a prime-time show. A storyboard looks like a comic strip with nothing drawn in any of the little squares. As the producers work on the show they fill in the squares, sketching in the performers so everyone can "see" how the action will flow from moment to moment.

You certainly don't have to attempt storyboards for your wedding, but use your imagination to build a step-by-step pageant. The trip down the aisle is the most dramatic part of the event, but the possibilities are virtually limitless. Include the pre-wedding parties, the toasts, the first dance, the cutting of the cake, and the tossing of the bouquet and the garter. Make it all work for you. Chapter 2 will describe each element of this pageant in detail.

▼ *The Concept worksheet can be found on pages 190–91.*

▲▲▲▲▲▲▲

THE
CEREMONY

▼▼▼▼▼▼▼

2

T H E   C E R E M O N Y

Weddings have come down to us through the centuries subdivided into religious and nonreligious groupings. Whether your plan includes a religious or a civil ceremony, there are three distinct phases to any wedding. You should get to know just what you have to work with:

1) the announcement of the upcoming wedding and the preparations for the event;

2) the religious or civil ceremony that makes it all legal;

3) a post-ceremony celebration.

Of the above, you have complete control over numbers one and three. The sky's the limit, and you can make these as expansive or discreet as you choose. Number two, the actual ceremony, is pretty much orchestrated for you as it has been for millions of couples reaching back through the years.

There is some flexibility, however, in the actual presentation of the religious and civil services. Almost every minister, priest, rabbi, or official adds his or her own personal touch and/or interpretation to the ceremony. And within the last decade many of the world's major religions have relaxed their rules about the actual service, allowing couples to insert material of their own choosing. The extras are often delivered by lay persons—a wonderful opportunity to include loved ones in this important event. If you would like to make additions, bring the material you've selected when you go to the planning meeting with the clergy.

At the planning meeting you will be clued in on how your wedding ceremony is put together. In the meantime, here are the basics of each type of service:

PROTESTANT

The general order of service for the Protestant wedding ceremony is presented here under the guidance of the Reverend John O. Mellin, pastor of the First Presbyterian Church of New York City. Mr. Mellin has included a relatively new portion of the service in which the minister asks the members of the congregation if they will make a commitment to "create a community in which this new family may grow in God's peace and joy." The congregation then answers, "We do."

The Protestant service is as follows:

a) The clergyman makes the statement of the meaning and purpose of Christian marriage, which is followed by a prayer.

b) The clergyman asks the bride and groom if they take each other to be lawfully wedded wife/husband.

c) The clergyman asks who is giving the bride away; the bride-giver identifies himself or herself and then leaves the altar and joins the congregation.

d) The bride and groom each repeat the wedding vows as directed by the clergyman, and the wedding ring or rings are given.

e) The members of the congregation are asked if they will make a commitment to be supportive to the new family.

f) Following prayers, including the Lord's Prayer, the clergyman charges that "those whom God has joined together let no man put asunder." The wedding is concluded with a benediction.

CATHOLIC

This order of service is based on the Roman Ritual revised by decree of the Second Vatican Ecumenical Council and published by the authority of Pope Paul VI. One party of the couple must be Catholic, and the couple must meet with a priest for wedding preparations.

There are three parts to a Catholic wedding service: the entrance rite, the liturgy of the word, and the liturgy of the eucharist or Mass. A nuptial Mass is appropriate only if both bride and groom are Catholics.

The general order of service for a Catholic wedding is as follows:

a) entrance rite; prayers by the priest;

b) liturgy of the word; readings from the Old and New Testaments; a reading from the Gospel;

c) homily, or sermon, in which the priest relates the gospel to everyday life;

THE CEREMONY

d) rite of marriage:

    1) instructions from the priest;

    2) statement of intention—priest asks and couple responds;

    3) consent:

        i) led by the priest, the couple consent to wed each other;

        ii) the priest, representing the Church, receives the consent;

e) wedding ring or rings blessed and given;

f) if no Mass is to be celebrated, the priest offers prayers of general intercession and closes with the nuptial blessing;

g) if both bride and groom are Catholic, a Nuptial Mass may be celebrated.

JEWISH

Jewish ceremonies can be Reformed, Conservative, or Orthodox, depending on the beliefs of the bridal couple and their families. According to Helene Ferris, Associate Rabbi of the Stephen Wise Free Synagogue in New York City, a typical traditional order of service might be as follows:

a) Service begins with assorted blessings, addresses, and/or vocal selections.

b) The rabbi offers the groom the cup of wine.

c) The bride and groom each repeat the wedding vow, as directed by the rabbi.

d) Wedding ring(s) are exchanged.

e) The marriage document (Ketubah), which is usually signed before the ceremony, is read aloud by the rabbi.

f) The seven marriage blessings are chanted.

g) The second cup of wine is presented to the couple, and the rabbi pronounces them husband and wife.

h) Following the benediction, a wineglass is shattered, and the congregation wishes the couple *Mazel Tov.*

CIVIL CEREMONY

The order of service for a civil ceremony varies from state to state. It can be conducted by any official acknowledged by that state government to be legally able to perform it, and usually the ceremony is incredibly brief. If you are planning a private civil ceremony, be sure to discuss the wording with the person who will perform the marriage. You may want to insert some more personal material into the ceremony or at least check out how he or she plans to do it.

If you are going to be married at your local city hall, find out when you go to get your marriage license how the ceremony is usually conducted.

Each of the major religions has its own timing for marriage ceremonies. Traditionally, Protestant weddings are not held on Sundays or on Good Friday. Catholic weddings may be held any day except Good Friday and are always scheduled before seven p.m. except in dire emergencies. Jewish weddings are not held on Shabbat and other major holy days.

Most Protestant clergymen will perform religious wedding ceremonies in locations outside the church and will co-officiate with other clerics. Many Catholic dioceses prohibit religious marriage ceremonies from taking place outside the church. Under certain circumstances an interfaith marriage may take place in a Catholic church with a minister or rabbi as an assisting celebrant. The consent of the local bishop is needed if a priest wishes to participate in a wedding in a non-Catholic church.

Jewish rabbis will perform marriage ceremonies outside the synagogue. Orthodox and Conservative rabbis do not officiate at mixed marriages; some Reform rabbis will also refuse. Marriages of divorced persons create problems for most clergymen. In other words, check your priest, minister, or rabbi very early in the planning and find out what possibilities are available to you.

If you want to have a religious ceremony in a church or synagogue, make the reservation immediately after you have set the date. Many places are booked months ahead, especially in the spring and fall, so don't wait. Also, most churches and synagogues have their own rules as to flowers, decorations, candles, photography, and music. Equipment such as candelabra and flower urns may be available for rental. Since all this might well affect the rest of your wedding planning, be smart and get the facts as soon as you can.

You will meet with your clergyman at least once before the wedding rehearsal, so you may want to photocopy the checklist on page 194 and bring it to the meeting in order to get all the necessary information in good, usable form.

If you opt for a religious ceremony in your home or in a party space, you will need to spend a bit more time organizing it. Your efforts will replace the church or temple backup staff who handle weddings all year round. Here are some points to discuss with your clergyman:

a) layout of space: this is best done by bringing a copy of the floor plan you will make, using the directions in Chapter 5, Location. The clergyman will want to see the location of the "altar" space, aisles, and so forth;

b) costs: how and when he or she would like to be paid;

c) traditional service and additional options (see above);

d) preferences as to photography, videotaping, and any pageantry you would like to include, such as bride's carpet, aisle ribbons, candlelight, and so forth;

e) music: outline what you would like to do and get suggestions on possible programs. If you wish to use soloists or musicians, ask for recommendations;

f) timing: schedule the rehearsal and work out the timing for the wedding day.

If a civil ceremony seems more logical for you, allow plenty of time to locate and select the official you want to perform the ceremony. This is a bit tricky since there is no registry or directory for people who can officiate at weddings. Each state has its own definition of who may perform marriage ceremonies. Personal recommendations are the surest way to find an official, so ask friends to ask friends. If nobody can come up with names, check your lawyer. Most states include judges, sheriffs, and other legal persons in their lists of officials who can perform wedding ceremonies. It's up to you to find an official who will bring to the ceremony all the good feelings you want, rather than a split-second exchange of curt words.

Don't hesitate to shop around until you find an official you feel is really right. Consider it a casting call for one of the lead roles in the wedding pageant—not

THE CEREMONY

everyone will fit the part as you see it played. Once you've made your selection, go over your floor plan and music presentation with the official so he or she understands exactly what you want to have happen. And be sure to discuss the actual wording of the ceremony plus any additional material you and/or the official would like to include. You don't want any surprises on the Big Day.

▲▲▲▲▲▲▲

SAFEGUARDING YOUR SPECIAL DAY

▼▼▼▼▼▼▼

All the above plans will be made much in advance of your wedding day to reserve for you the place, the person, and the ceremony you want. However, a word of caution. Even though everything seems set, you should make a phone call the week before the wedding just to double-check the schedule of the clergyman or official. Events occur, people's health changes, and things can get completely fouled up.

Let me tell you about my friends Bob and Ellen Delgado who planned a sensational garden wedding at a friend's isolated country house. As good Catholics they wanted a religious ceremony but needed to locate a priest who would officiate outside a holy sanctuary. Through friends of friends they located a maverick priest active in the peace movement who had performed similar ceremonies. They made all the arrangements with him in-

cluding scheduling a brief rehearsal several hours before the guests were to arrive. The only thing they didn't do was double-check.

The day was perfect. The tent was in place, the caterer had arrived, the florist had delivered, and two hundred guests were headed for rural South Jersey when Bob and Ellen discovered that their priest was several states away in a demonstration. There was no way he could make it, and it was too late to reschedule the wedding.

One of the ushers was an actor who had played character roles including priests, so some members of the wedding party were all for dressing him up in clerical collar and continuing with the day as planned. The rest of the attendants were horrified and leaped into cars to scour the countryside for somebody—anybody—who could perform a wedding. And Bob and Ellen assured each other that, come what may, they would have a religious ceremony in the near future.

The car contingent lucked out and found the mayor of a nearby town who agreed to perform the marriage. The ceremony was a little late, a little impersonal, and a bit breathless, but the day was saved. Then, months later, when the religious ceremony was to take place in the vestry of a local Catholic church, everybody showed up only to find that that priest had forgotten the appointment and had gone to visit his mother upstate. "How was the wedding?" his mother inquired. "What wedding?" he asked, and then said, "Ohhhh noooo..." as he grabbed his coat.

▼ *The Ceremony Checklist can be found on pages 194–95.*

▲▲▲▲▲▲▲▲

PLANNING YOUR BUDGET AND SELECTING YOUR CEREMONY

▼▼▼▼▼▼▼

3

PLANNING YOUR BUDGET
AND CEREMONY

Planning your budget allocations takes precedence over all wedding activities at this point. Begin by arriving at a figure both of you agree to spend on the total celebration. If parents or other near-and-dears are putting up some of the ▼▼▼▼▼▼ money, they must be consulted about their contributions as rapidly as you can arrange to do so. Getting the backing for this show is top priority. Even though most of us are a bit hesitant to talk money, if you can get it out of the way immediately your life will be simpler.

Weddings are notoriously runaway expensive. By setting your "bottom line" right at the very beginning and vowing to stick to it, you can control the potential runaway and get a lot more value out of each dollar.

Years ago, before women were liberated, all but a few wedding expenses were divided into what the bride's father had to pay for and what the groom (or his father) had to pay for. Strict accounting was suggested. It worked out as follows.

The bride's father paid for:

All announcements, invitations, and mailing costs

All photography

Bride's premarital blood test

Bride's wedding dress and trousseau

Rental of church or synagogue, if any

Fees for organist or musicians, sexton, parking policeman, and so forth

Decorations and flowers for sanctuary

Bride's carpet, aisle ribbons

Bridesmaids' bouquets

Bridesmaids' luncheon

Gifts for attendants

Transportation of bridal party from home to ceremony and to reception

Groom's ring, if any

Accommodations for bridal attendants, if needed

Entire wedding reception

The groom or his father paid for:

Groom's blood test and the marriage license

Bride's rings

Bride's bouquet and boutonnieres for groomsmen

Corsages for mothers and bride's going-away corsage

Gloves and ties for groomsmen

Gifts for groomsmen

Rehearsal dinner

Clergyman's fee

Accommodations for groomsmen, if needed

Accommodations for groom's family, if needed

Wedding trip

Attendants paid for:

Their wedding clothes

Travel expenses to bride's home

Fortunately, today's bride and groom can do pretty much as they please about sharing the expenses, since most have jobs or careers bringing in independent income. The old saying, "Money brings money," certainly applies; the most effective way to discuss funding this event is to begin by announcing how much each of you plans to contribute!

Once you have set the amount, begin to use the workbook budget pages. You may find it helpful to remove them to photocopy several times so each of you has a set to work with. Make staying within the budget a priority.

The major budget categories are:

Location
Invitations and postage
Clothing
Flowers
Decorations
Food and food service
Beverages and beverage service
Sound and music
Lighting
Photography

Each workbook budget page is set up so that you can write in your overall budget figure for that category prominently on top. Below are spaces for the things you might need to spend money on within that category. As you get firm quotes, settle on rentals, or are offered things for free, fill in the sheets, subtracting the committed amounts from the totals.

Every week or so go over the budget pages to see if you need to refocus. This periodic adjustment is standard procedure in preproduction theater budgeting and will work for you. In fact, it's the only way to keep firm control over your money.

When "extra" money shows up in one category, you'll know it early enough to tuck it into another category that seems wanting. By keeping your accounting up to the minute you gain flexibility, keep the overall sense of proportion, and acquire a little serenity besides.

▲▲▲▲▲▲▲

HOW IT ALL GOES TOGETHER

▼▼▼▼▼▼▼

Now you're probably curious about how it all goes together. Let's start with the space in which the wedding ceremony will be held. One end of that space must be designated as the focal point, in front of which all the action takes place. Religious sanctuaries will already have the focal point, that is, the altar, built in. For rented or residential space you can decide where to place the focal point. (More about this in Chapter 11, Decor and Props.)

Be it church, synagogue, garden, living room, or rented party space, it will be divided in half. Looking at it as you face the "altar," the left side is for the bride's guests and the right for the groom's. If the space has no main aisle, draw an imaginary line down the middle of the seating area, designating the left for the bride and the right for the groom.

When the guests arrive for the ceremony they are escorted to seats beginning with the middle and going to the rear of the space, with the groom's friends seated on the right and the bride's guests on the left.

The bride's immediate family is escorted to the very front pews or seats on the left side, and the groom's family is placed at the front on the right side. In formal weddings these front pews or seats are designated as "reserved," and no other guests are seated with the family. At less formal ceremonies close friends of the family may share the front pews. When the ceremony is over, the rest of the guests remain in place after the reces-

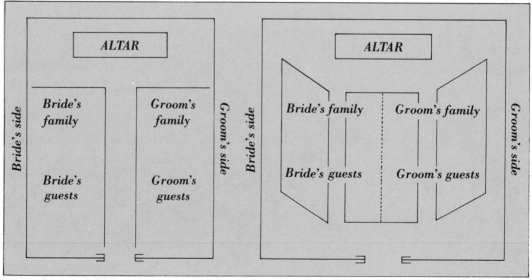

Floor plan of wedding room

sional until both immediate families have followed the wedding procession back down the aisle.

The bride has her attendants; the groom, his. The bride's group may include the following:

bridesmaids—as many or as few as you want. Incidentally, the "maids" don't have to be maidens; married girlfriends are fine

maid of honor—truly a Miss

matron of honor—truly a Mrs.

flower girl—more than one if you like

The groom's group may include the following:

best man

ring bearer

page—as many as you want

ushers—perhaps the same number as there are bridesmaids. Operationally, figure that you'll need one usher for every thirty-five to forty guests

In addition there may be generic helpers:

candlelighters

program distributors

doormen

hymnbook passers

In Christian ceremonies the bride is traditionally given away by her father or some older, meaningful male friend. In most Jewish ceremonies both parents accompany both the bride and the groom down the aisle. (See worksheets at the back of the book for diagrams of Christian and Jewish processionals and recessionals and record-keeping space for your attendant choices.) If there is no one appropriate to give the bride away, she may walk down the aisle alone in her proper place in the processional.

The walk down the aisle is not mandatory; it is merely a terrific way to stage the pageantry of the wedding ceremony. Older brides and brides who are remarrying occasionally choose to skip the aisle walk and enter either with their groom or solo from a side entrance at the front of the space near the altar.

The **bridesmaids** are more decorative than functional. They follow the ushers in the wedding procession, walking in pairs toward the altar. At the altar they turn to the left and stand to the far left, leaving space for the rest of the bride's party. For the recessional, they pair off with the ushers and are the last to go down the aisle. The bridesmaids add to the romantic pageantry, echoing an ancient tradition of handmaidens, ladies in waiting, maidens of the village, and so forth. As for their dramatic value, a bevy of young beauties decked out in finery adds a wonderful touch to almost any production.

A **junior bridesmaid** is a rarely used category of attendant that might be helpful to you if there is a young teenage girl who is seriously pining to be in the wedding. Too old to be a flower girl and too young to be a bridesmaid (that is, a peer friend of the bride), the junior bridesmaid gets to dress like the bridesmaids and holds similar flowers. She walks alone directly before the maid and matron of honor in the processional and before the maid and matron of honor and their usher/best man escorts in the recessional.

If there is a young man counterpart who can be talked into being in the wedding party to escort the junior bridesmaid, you can make him a **junior usher,** dressed like the rest of the groomsmen. He would walk in front of the ushers in the processional and escort the junior bridesmaid in the recessional. Again, this is not usual but is available to you if needed.

The **maid and matron of honor,** if you choose to have both, are more functional. Select one of them to participate in the ceremony as the bride's helper and to witness the signing of the wedding certificate. Both the maid and the matron will precede the bride down the aisle. The one designated as helper will carry the groom's ring if there is to be a double ring exchange, hold the bride's bouquet when the groom places the ring on her finger, and lift the bride's veil for the ceremonial kiss. She walks out in the recessional on the arm of the best man. At the end of the reception she helps the bride change clothes and prepare to go away. And, most often, she will hostess a pre-wedding festivity such as a bridal shower.

The **flower girl,** if any, is also functional as well as decorative. She will be prepubescent, anywhere from six to ten or so, and probably adorable. She walks directly in front of the bride and bride's father in the processional, and directly after the bride and groom in the recessional. Her job, theoretically, is to toss rose petals in the path of the bride. Alas, many churches have banned the use of real flower petals since they can get dangerously slippery. Some churches allow paper rose petals as a substitute, however, or the child may walk in the procession holding a pretty little basket of flowers. It's a wonderful touch.

The **best man** is the groom's helper, witnessing the signing of the wedding cer-

tificate. He enters the church with the groom, stands with him at the altar, and holds the wedding ring if there is no ring bearer. He pays the clergyman, using money furnished by the groom. At the reception he sits to the right of the bride and is responsible for proposing the first toast to the married couple. He may organize and introduce other toasts following his and reads aloud all telegrams and good wishes that arrive for the newlyweds. The best man often drives the get-away car and is supposed to shield the couple from postwedding pranks.

The **ring bearer** or **page** is the counterpart of the flower girl, an adorable six- to ten-year-old whose function is to carry a small, decorative pillow onto which the wedding ring is securely tied. He walks directly in front of the flower girl in the processional and directly after her in the recessional. At the appropriate moment in the ceremony he offers the pillow to the best man who undoes the ring and passes it to the groom.

The **ushers** have a lot to do. The groom selects one usher to be the head usher, responsible for overseeing the rest of the group. The head usher gives out the boutonnieres and directs the lighting of the candles, the hanging of the aisle ribbons, and the laying of the bride's carpet, if any of these are used, before the ceremony begins.

He personally ushers in the groom's parents and the bride's mother. He makes sure the ushers line up for duty at the wedding room door and offer their *left arm* to the eldest lady in each group of guests, while inquiring whether the guests are to be seated on the bride's side or the groom's side. Arms are never offered to male guests. The other guests in each party follow the usher and the eldest lady down the aisle to be seated.

Ushers walk in pairs, leading off the processional. At the altar they turn and walk to the far right side, standing close to the groom and best man. In the recessional, each usher pairs off with a bridesmaid and escorts her down the aisle, finishing up the wedding party.

Aisle ribbons and a bride's carpet are charming customs you may choose to include in your pageantry if your wedding room space permits. At a home wedding, the ribbons and carpet add a pleasant bit of formality, helping to turn the living room into a special, ceremonial place. They are easy to make or can be rented from the church or a local florist. They are put in place by the ushers just before the processional is to begin.

If your ceremony is to be a religious one in a sanctuary, be sure to discuss ribbons and carpets with your clergyman before you put effort and money into them. While not exactly controversial, ribbons and carpets are viewed as slightly frivolous by some religious groups.

If a bride's carpet is used, it is unfurled just before the ceremony begins. The carpet, usually made of thin white canvas or linen, is in place before the guests arrive, neatly accordion pleated on the floor directly in front of the altar. Immediately after the bride's mother is seated, the sanctuary doors are closed. Then two ushers, or the head usher and one other, go to the carpet, pick up a corner each, and walk slowly back down the main aisle toward the entry, pulling the carpet with them to form a special pathway for the wedding party. When the carpet is in

place, the music begins and the procession starts down the aisle. The carpet is not removed until after everyone has left the wedding room.

The aisle ribbons may be put in place right after or before the bride's carpet, depending on the customs of the church. The clergyman will outline the accepted procedure when you have your prenuptial meeting. For a home wedding, schedule them in whichever order makes the most sense to you. The ribbons generally are wide satin bands long enough to reach to the back of the room, either from the altar or from the first unreserved pews. They are usually white but may be color coordinated to the wedding party.

There is a lot of latitude with aisle ribbons. Some churches use plain wide ribbons that are placed, neatly folded, on the floor next to the front pews. At the appropriate moment two ushers take the ribbons and walk them back toward the entry, laying the ribbon over the backs of the pews next to the aisle. If the pews have posts, small ribbon loops may be sewn onto the ends of each ribbon, and the loops are slipped over the posts on the ends of the aisle sides of the first and last pews, to hold it securely.

Other churches permit decorated ribbons, complete with bows, streamers, and small flowers sewn on in clusters, at the points that the ribbon touches the back of each pew. Small ribbon loops are sewn on at each cluster, to be slipped over the end post of each pew as the ushers walk the ribbons back toward the sanctuary entrance. The bulk of the decorated aisle ribbons makes folding them on the floor rather unfeasible; rather, all the loops are carefully hung over the end post of the

29

Aisle ribbons

very front pews and form a pretty frame through which the wedding procession passes en route to the altar. At home, use aisle chairs with appropriate backs and hang the ribbons on the chair backs by means of small ribbon loops.

If reserved pews are designated, the ribbons are hung from the last reserved pew and stretched back to the entry. Following the recessional the immediate families leave and then the ushers gather up the ribbons, releasing the rest of the guests. The aisle ribbons effectively pen in the congregation until after the recessional. This works to good advantage when a reception line is held at the entrance to the sanctuary; the extra minutes are often needed to get the reception line organized.

Once you have made your selection (that is, cast all the roles) photocopy these pages and give the participants a copy of what they will be expected to do. For your own peace of mind, use the workbook pages, filling in each person's name next to the stick figure place in the processional diagrams. Mentally play with the positioning of the attendants, creating the best visual grouping you can come up with. Try to "see" how your procession will look making its way down the aisle. If this is done rather early on, the wedding rehearsal becomes a smoother, easier session.

▼ *The Processional worksheets can be found on pages 196–99.*

▲▲▲▲▲▲▲

PROTOCOL

▼▼▼▼▼▼▼

4

P R O T O C O L

▼ ▼ ▼ *n this chapter we're going to take a look at the chronological se-*
quence of events that are traditionally included in the overall cele-
bration. Ideally they are spread out over six months or so. You may
decide to go for all of them, or you may select from the list. Once
you've decided what you are going to include, use the workbook
pages to establish a calendar and organize the work so your events are fun
and run smoothly.

Many of the activities listed below involve party giving. Use the informa-
tion in the chapters on food and beverage service for help in entertaining
groups of people. A good party is a good party, no matter what its purpose!

▲▲▲▲▲▲▲

ANNOUNCING YOUR ENGAGEMENT

▼▼▼▼▼▼▼

As soon as you decide to get married you'll probably want to tell everybody. Restrain yourselves. Protocol demands that both sets of parents be told first, which makes sense. Think of how hurt your parents would be if they learned through the grapevine of your momentous decision! However you do it, tell the parents immediately, and then you are free to tell your friends, who probably knew it was going to happen all along.

Shortly after you tell your parents, you'll need to introduce them to each other if they are not acquainted. By marrying you are establishing a relationship between two families. Since the relationship will continue until death do you part, make the introductions as pleasant as possible.

A food-oriented occasion is selected most often to introduce the parents. Limit the guest list to you and them only. If any of the parents are divorced, separated, remarried, and so forth, you may be better off planning separate gatherings rather than throwing them all in together. Be as sensitive as you can. The old jokes about gaining/losing a son/daughter are based on fears, illogical but painful.

Try having something casual: a brunch, a luncheon, cocktails at a favorite place, whatever suits your style. If you invite them out rather than to your place, you must pick up the tab. You might need to arrange this discreetly with the waiter long before the check is presented to avoid the party ending in competitive check-grabbing.

Keep it simple, keep it brief in case everybody hates one another, and spend a little time researching possible topics of conversation. Everyone is going to be nervous, them as well as you, so figure out how to bring out the best in each person.

▲▲▲▲▲▲▲

THE ENGAGEMENT PARTY

▼▼▼▼▼▼▼

A formal engagement party can be held anytime after the parents are informed. Traditionally, the bride's family gives the engagement party. If the groom's parents are the only local set, however, or if they have the most logical facilities, discuss the possibility of their hosting the party with the bride's family. If the plan pleases everybody, go ahead. If no parents are available, an engagement party can be given by close friends.

You have a wide range of parties to choose from. Whatever type of entertainment you really enjoy is fine, from a barbecue to a dinner dance. The main point to remember is that sometime during the event a formal toast to the engaged couple is proposed by the host or hostess, glasses clink, best wishes are offered, and the engagement is thus made "official."

You or your hostess may choose to send out invitations that state "engagement party" on them, or have matchbooks and cocktail napkins imprinted with the bride and groom's names. There are all kinds of props available from party stores for engagement parties. No props are necessary, but feel free to include any that catch your fancy.

The big behind-the-scenes benefit you gain from having an engagement party is that both of you, and all the relatives, are motivated to begin pulling together the guest list you'll need for the wedding. For total efficiency, the list should go on three-by-five file cards and include everything—titles and zip codes. Alphabetize the cards and get a little file card box for safekeeping. Social secretaries have been doing this for years because it really works. If your time is tight, perhaps somebody would like to volunteer to be your wedding social secretary.

A personal computer can simplify this process if one is available to you. Create an alphabetized wedding guest file, entering all pertinent data: name, complete address, telephone, and number of people in party. Once entered, you can easily run off copies of the list for friends who are helping you address envelopes and for hosts and hostesses of showers and pre-wedding parties. (It will also serve well as your Christmas card list for the next few years.)

As responses come in, input them, and if gifts are received, note the date received, a description of the gift, and the date you sent your thank-you note. Incorporate bridal shower data, if gifts are received and thank-you's sent. It's a wonderful timesaving way to keep track of everything!

Announcing your engagement via the newspapers is done to coincide with the engagement party, or it can substitute for an engagement party. Please refer to Chapter 13, Photography, for data on writing and sending out press releases and photos.

If your engagement is announced in the local papers, you will probably begin receiving mail from department stores and gift shops suggesting you utilize their bridal registries. If no such mail appears, telephone and ask, because registries are often a big help to people who want to send you something marvelous but don't know your personal tastes. They offer a socially acceptable way of asking for the gifts you really want to receive.

The service is free and can be fun. Shop the stores that have a bridal registry, choose what you like, and have the store list your preferences for your friends and acquaintances. Tell everybody the stores with which you are registered so they can ask about your selections when they shop. If you have chosen china, silver, and crystal patterns, the registry is a great way to fill in your patterns.

▲▲▲▲▲▲▲▲

SHOWERS

▼▼▼▼▼▼▼

Between the engagement party and the week before the wedding is the time for a bridal shower. There may be one or several, depending on the circumstances. Traditionally, the maid or matron of honor is the hostess for a shower, but any friend or relative can give you one. In some parts of the country the immediate family is considered taboo for shower giving. The purpose of a shower is to collect gifts for the couple, stocking their new household with necessities and luxuries. If the immediate family holds a shower, it may smack of greed, so check out the local customs.

Sometimes showers are surprise parties; sometimes the bridal couple is asked what kinds of gifts are needed and a specific shower (that is, kitchen or linens) may be planned. Years ago the "naughty lingerie" shower was a favorite with close girlfriends. Be prepared to say what you want if asked. Be prepared also to offer your hostess your guest list, with complete addresses. Here's where those alphabetized cards and/or computer files begin to show their worth! Suggest to your hostess that she pass on to the guests the names of the stores where you have registered so that guests can use the bridal registry if they need help on gift selection.

As to the type of party, a shower can be anything the hostess chooses, from a pleasant coffee hour to a sit-down dinner. It can be all female or include the gentlemen, or the men can join the ladies after an hour or two. The only rule on shower guests is to be sure they are also invited to the wedding. If they are visiting from far away, they must be sent the wedding announcement the day after the wedding.

Before the gifts are opened be sure to ask one of the guests to be the record keeper, writing down a brief description of each gift and the name of the giver. Even though you're positive you'll remember every wonderful detail, get the written list as your backup. Haven't all of us received awkward thank-you notes that uneasily avoid mentioning exactly what the gift was? It's lack of a backup list every time.

Many charming customs surround bridal showers. The bride's fortune cake is served in many parts of the country and can be delightful. Small, well wrapped favors from the dime store are inserted into the cake or placed between the layers so the guests may find their "fortune" in their portion. Favors usually include the following:

Coin . . . . riches
Ring . . . . next person married
Thimble . . . . old maid
Four-leaf clover . . . luck
Boat or plane . . . . . travel
Heart . . . . romance
Dagger . . . . intrigue

Add anything you can think of to the above list or do your own set of favors hand-tailored to your guest list. Be sure to caution guests that favors are in the cake; avoid dental catastrophes!

New Haven party consultant Mickey Balaban, who is affiliated with a major hotel chain, tells of the bridal bonnet, another country-wide custom that's fun and silly. As the bride unwraps each gift somebody takes the wrapping and uses some part of the paper or ribbon from every gift to create a hat that the bride then wears for the rest of the party. The more exotic the better since it's a perfect photo opportunity.

▲▲▲▲▲▲▲

BRIDESMAIDS' LUNCHEON

▼▼▼▼▼▼▼

This is somewhat of a misnomer. A more accurate title would be "Planning Session for the Bride's Attendants plus the Mothers of the Bride, Groom, Flower Girl, and Ring Bearer If They Are Available." It's an important meeting, luncheon or no,

PROTOCOL

and should be scheduled as soon as everyone you want to be in the wedding has accepted.

This is where you tell everybody how you envision the wedding and discuss what you would like them all to wear. It's also a fine time to recruit volunteers for the costume department. More important, it offers you, the bride, your first chance to assert your authority over the entire ensemble.

Control is a mixed blessing, but we presume you will handle it gracefully. You know and your attendants know that there is no one cut of garment that looks terrific on everybody or one hat style that flatters every face. Yet you will probably want all your attendants to dress similarly for the sake of the total visual effect. And you will want the mothers to understand what you're aiming for so they will give you cooperation rather than a hard time. Remember, the producer has the final word on any show, and you are the producers.

Expect to work hard selling your production concept to all concerned and be ready to compromise a bit. You might begin with a description of the overall feeling you want to create, harkening back to the conceptualizing you did in Chapter 1. Then use the information in Chapter 7, Costumes, to show how you hope to carry out your concept. Bring your fabric swatches, sketches, or patterns for the gowns and accessories along to the luncheon. Aim for enthusiasm, and hope for the best.

Also bring photocopies of the appropriate processional pages from the workbook section and get everybody to write in their sizes for everything, plus addresses and home and work telephone numbers.

THE BACHELOR PARTY

The most important point about the bachelor party: Make sure it is not scheduled for the night before the wedding! This legendary bash is supposed to celebrate the groom's leave-taking from the randy pleasures of bachelorhood. It sometimes takes several days for the groom and his buddies to recover from the effects of the party, so schedule it early in the week before the wedding.

The best man and the ushers organize the bachelor party and generally exclude all females. The fathers of the bride and groom are often included, resulting in occasional culture shock. The party officially begins with the groom proposing a toast to the bride. It can go anywhere from there.

In contrast to the bride's fortune cake and the bridal bonnet, there seems to be only one custom that appears all over the country at bachelor parties—a scantily clad lady jumps out of a large cardboard cake. New York scenic artist Jill Tannone designed and built such a cake for us. Her directions for cake making are included in Chapter 11, Decor and Props.

THE WEDDING REHEARSAL AND REHEARSAL DINNER

The evening before the ceremony is usually the best time for the wedding rehearsal since everybody in the procession must be there, and the rehearsal must be held in the space where the ceremony will be performed. Try to include the processional and recessional music at the rehearsal so everybody can practice walking in time to the beat. If this is a religious ceremony, the clergyman will officiate as director. If not, appoint the mother of the bride or one of the groom's parents to direct the action. Also, refer to the processional and recessional diagrams on pages 196 to 199.

The actual wedding should duplicate the rehearsal. On the wedding day, however, a few extra details must be taken care of that will not be rehearsed; for example, before the ceremony the groom and best man meet with the clergyman who checks the marriage license, receives his or her fee, and makes sure the best man has the ring. Arrange these extras at the rehearsal.

The sequence for the Christian ceremony is as follows:

Background music begins thirty minutes before ceremony

Backstage, the clergyman meets with the groom and best man, receives his fee, checks the marriage license, and sees that the best man has the ring

Ushers begin seating guests

Groom's mother and father are shown in by head usher

Bride's mother is shown in by head usher five minutes before ceremony is to begin

Ushers or candlelighters light candles

Aisle ribbons and/or carpet are placed by ushers

Clergyman enters and goes to altar

Groom and best man come from side room and stand at right side of altar

Processional music starts

Bride's mother rises, indicating everyone should stand

Processional (use the workbook diagram); rule of thumb for spacing: keep each person or persons four pews apart as they go down the aisle

Ceremony

Recessional (use the workbook diagram)

Ushers escort bridesmaids out. If aisle ribbons are used, two ushers reenter the church via a side aisle and then remove the aisle ribbons. If a side aisle is unavailable, they may return via the main aisle to remove the ribbons.

Head usher escorts bride's mother out; bride's father follows them

Groom's mother is escorted out, followed by groom's father

Ushers continue removing the aisle ribbons and releasing the crowd

If some of the audience is not invited to the reception, a receiving line is formed at the door

A double wedding follows the same general order, with the older bride preceding and participating in the ceremony before the younger bride. If the brides are sisters, generally the eldest is escorted by her father, and the younger by a close male friend or relative. The father may choose, however, to escort both brides down, one on each arm, if the wedding aisle is wide enough to accommodate everybody. If the brides are not sisters, each is escorted by her own father or appropriate man.

If the church or synagogue has two aisles, both bridal parties may enter at the same time and meet in front of the altar. This, obviously, takes much tighter timing to make sure it doesn't look like a straggly crowd scene, so allow an extra half hour at the rehearsal to have several run-throughs.

The processional and recessional in a double wedding are modified also. In the processional, all the ushers (that is, both brides' ushers) lead off in pairs, followed by the bridal attendants of the elder bride and then the elder bride on her father's arm. Next come the bridal attendants of the younger bride, finishing with the younger bride on her escort's arm. The recessional is led by the elder bride and groom, followed by the younger bride and groom and then all the attendants, paired off as in a single wedding.

Two reception lines may be formed if the brides are not sisters. In the rest of the reception protocol, the elder bride and her groom go first, followed by the younger bride and her groom.

The sequence for Jewish ceremonies varies according to whether the couple is Reformed, Conservative, or Orthodox. Your rabbi will be your authority here, making sure your ceremony conforms to the customs of your faith. Much of the sequence for a Christian wedding applies to a traditional Jewish ceremony, except that the bride and groom each may march down the aisle, accompanied by both parents. Refer to the processional and recessional diagrams at the back of this book.

The receiving line order, whether at the church or at the reception, is as follows:

Mother of the bride
Father of the groom
Mother of the groom
Father of the bride
Bride
Groom
(Optional: maid/matron and brides-
maids)

If everybody is going to the reception, the wedding party goes out the door and straight into cars to be driven away.

(It is suggested that you photocopy the above for on-site use.)

Following the rehearsal it's customary to have a dinner or luncheon hosted by the groom's parents. The bride and groom are seated at the head of the table. The groom's father proposes the first toast—to the entire company. Sometime during the party the attendants are each given a small personal gift as a thank-you and as a memento. The gifts are always prettily wrapped and are generally opened immediately.

▲▲▲▲▲▲▲▲

THE RECEPTION

▼▼▼▼▼▼▼

Protocol for the reception might strike you as a bit extraneous. The ceremony has been successfully completed, the bride is beautiful, the marriage is legal, and the partying can begin. Everybody can relax.

Well, almost. There happen to be a number of traditions built into the reception that make it different from any other party. Traditions, by definition, come down to us through the ages. Your parents, grand- and great-grandparents, and their parents before them kept the traditions, and now it's your turn. Years from now you may be prompting your own children on wedding reception etiquette. That's the way it is when you're a human.

In order to incorporate the reception traditions smoothly into your party somebody has to be in charge. Call him or her the director, stage manager, head person, or whatever. You need to appoint one person to organize the party and shepherd the guests from one event to another.

"People desire guidance," says Ken G. Deutsch, catering manager of San Francisco's Fairmont Hotel. "Guests come to celebrate a wonderful event. They want to forget their troubles and sorrows. By giving them positive direction you help them relax and have a good time.

"I arrange each wedding myself," Ken continues. "I'm afraid I'm a perfectionist. For generations Californians and guests across the country have said, 'There's nothing like a Fairmont wedding,' and I want to keep it that way! By working the party personally I can get the feel of the crowd. Then I'm able to pace the traditional events, speed things up when they slow down, lead applause when it's appropriate, cue the musicians, do whatever is needed to produce a beautiful event."

Ken's reputation for successful managing of Fairmont weddings follows a family tradition. In 1983 he replaced his uncle, Ted Deutsch, who was the legendary catering expert for thirty years!

Ken graciously consented to give us a chronological orchestration of how he runs a Fairmont reception. Use it as a worksheet for your appointed volunteer director, selecting the portions you like and want to include at your party. Focus on keeping the reception dramatic—this is a pageant, remember—and make sure your guests are never left wondering what to do next. If guests are comfortable and happy, the reception will be a success.

Here is the Fairmont wedding reception:

1) The music begins before any guests arrive. Happy sounds must greet the guests as they enter, setting the stage for a festive time. Musicians can range from a big band to strolling musicians. Use tapes and records if there are budgetary restrictions; however, there's nothing like live music to enhance a party.

2) If there has been no receiving line at the church or temple, the wedding party will be the first to arrive at the reception. Ken helps form the receiving line immediately, inside the entrance the guests will use, so the guests pass through the line on their way in to the party. The receiving line order, beginning with the first person to greet the entering guests, is as follows:

Mother of the bride
Father of the groom
Mother of the groom
Father of the bride
Bride
Groom

(The Fairmont lineup excludes the attendants in order to speed up the greetings.)

3) As each guest leaves the receiving line he or she moves into the cocktail part of the party. This may be held in the same room as the receiving line or in an adjacent space. Drinks are served, hors d'oeuvres are passed. The music continues and is appropriate for a cocktail party. There is no dancing yet.

4) Photographs are taken usually before or after the ceremony. If additional

PROTOCOL

pictures of the wedding party are needed, they may be taken after everybody has gone through the receiving line. Guests continue with cocktails. The photographer may be taking candid photos during the cocktail party. It's especially important to get all the relatives in the photos, so a family member should cue the photographer.

5) Ken signals his staff when cocktails are over, and the waiters discreetly tell the guests the food service is about to begin, directing them into the space that is set up for dining. No lights are flashed to signal the conclusion of the cocktail party; everything is done as elegantly and personally as possible. The music continues, furnishing pleasant background sound.

6) Depending on the time of day and the elaborateness of the wedding party, the food service might be sit-down or buffet.

7) The lights are dim as the guests are seated and are brought up for the entrance of the bridal couple. The bride and groom are held back to make their entrance. When most of the guests are seated, the music is softened, and Ken signals the announcer (normally the bandleader). Over the microphone the announcer asks the guests to welcome Mr. and Mrs._____ The musicians play "Here Comes the Bride," and Ken leads the applause as the couple enters and proceeds to the bride's table. Elaborately staged weddings include a follow spot, so the bride and groom are spotlighted, creating a very dramatic entrance to begin an elegant affair.

Bride's table

Bride ○   ○ Groom

Best man ○   ○ Maid of honor

Matron of honor ○   ○ Head usher

Usher ○   ○ Bridesmaid

Bridesmaid ○   ○ Usher

Usher ○   etc.   ○ Bridesmaid

If attendants have spouses they are seated at the bride's table also, following the male-female-male-female seating pattern.

Parents' table

Relative or friend ○   ○ Relative or friend

Clergyman ○   ○ Groom's mother

Bride's mother ○   ○ Bride's father

Groom's father ○   ○ Clergyman's wife

Relative or friend ○   etc.   ○ Relative or friend

Sample seating arrangements

8) Protocol for a Jewish wedding reception includes a blessing for the breaking of the bread. The rabbi or a distinguished guest might have been asked in advance if he or she would give the blessing. It is done as soon as the bride and groom are seated, and then the first course is served.

9) Bread blessing or no, at Ken's signal the best man stands and proposes a toast to the new Mr. and Mrs. In some families a ceremonial wedding cup is brought in, and the bride and groom drink to each other out of it. The cup is often an heirloom, ornately decorated, with two handles and a pedestal base. The couple link arms; each takes a handle and drinks more or less simultaneously, which takes a bit of practice.

10) The best man reads any telegrams, messages, and so forth, that have arrived and recognizes anyone else in the room who wants to propose a toast, say a few words, or read something he or she has written. This may also take place after the main course has been served, when everybody is more relaxed.

11) Following the toasts and so forth, the food service begins. The music continues as a background sound until about a third of the way through the first course, or the equivalent. Then Ken makes sure both sets of parents and the bridal party are available for the first dance. He alerts the photographer and signals the musicians who begin to play the bride and groom's favorite song. The lights are raised for the dance, then lowered afterward. The announcer says, "Now the bride and groom [names] will have their first dance."

There is protocol to the order of the dancing, and each change of partners offers a super photo opportunity so the dancers often have to stop and be photographed. The announcer gives the dance order, pacing it so it can be enjoyable as well as photographable. The order is as follows:

Bride and groom
Bride's parents
Groom's parents
(three couples on the floor)

Bride dances with her father
Groom dances with his mother-in-law
Groom's parents continue together

Bride dances with her father-in-law
Groom dances with his mother
Bride's parents dance together

The rest of the bridal party are invited to join the dance

The guests are invited to join the dance

12) If there is any reason why the dance sequence would be awkward for anyone (because of divorces, remarriages, and so forth), the parent participation is omitted and the bridal party is invited to dance as soon as the bride and groom are photographed.

13) "Now it's a party," says Ken. Dancing and the eating of the wedding feast continues. A non-wedding cake dessert concludes the food service, along with coffee. The Fairmont never uses the wedding cake as the dessert since it signifies the end of the party and people begin to leave.

14) Ken monitors the crowd to determine how long a break there should be between dinner and the cake cutting. He also controls the kitchen, synchronizes the band, times the serving of the food with the dancing—hot food must be served hot! When the main course is served, the band takes a break; a piano may supply background music.

At some point the party begins to slow down; that's the time to prepare for the cake presentation. Ken rounds up all the parents and the photographer, and alerts the musicians.

15) The Fairmont cake presentation is done dramatically. The cake is kept hidden until the right moment. The music fades and then comes up with "Here Comes the Bride" as the cake is wheeled into the middle of the room. If a follow spot is available, the cake is spotlighted. Again, the lights are raised for the cake and lowered after the cutting.

16) After the guests have had time to gather around, Ken places the bride and groom behind the cake, with the groom on the bride's left side. The groom holds the decorated cake knife in his right hand, and Ken places the bride's left hand on top of the groom's hand. As the photographer clicks away they pretend to cut the cake, slicing into the bottom tier only.

Lest the hand placement confuse you, it is done this way for the photographer. When the bride's left hand is on top, her beautiful rings will sparkle brightly for posterity!

17) Ken continues to cut the first piece of cake, places it on a cake plate, adds a fork, and hands it to the bride. She feeds a bite to the groom. Then the groom picks up a bit of cake in his fingers and feeds it to the bride. Ken has a napkin ready as soon as the photographer is fin-

ished! The cake is then wheeled back to the kitchen area, and the band starts playing "up," fast-dance music to get the party going again.

18) The bottom layers of the cake are served to the guests. The top layer is saved to be frozen and served on the first anniversary, along with a complimentary bottle of champagne, a nice touch to end a beautiful affair.

19) When the bride and groom are almost ready to leave, Ken organizes the throwing of the bride's bouquet. Again, photographer, parents, and attendants are alerted, and the announcer invites all the single women to participate. The musicians come up with a drum roll as she turns her back and throws the bouquet over her shoulder. Tradition has it that the woman who catches the bride's bouquet will be the next to wed.

20) Following the bouquet toss is the throwing of the garter, which the announcer invites the single men to catch. The groom removes the decorated garter the bride is wearing just below her knee, turns, and tosses it over his shoulder. The garter ceremony has drum roll accompaniment and is supposed to forecast which man will be next to wed.

21) The finale is the going away, when the bride and groom leave the party and symbolically leave their families to begin married life. Guests are often offered little bags of confetti to toss at the couple as they dash to the get-away car, traditionally driven by the best man.

Ken adds, "Remember, every wedding is different. No two are alike. It's your day—enjoy it to the fullest!"

▼ *The Calendar worksheets can be found on pages 192–93.*

▲▲▲▲▲▲▲

LOCATIONS

▼▼▼▼▼▼▼

5

LOCATIONS

T he search for the perfect place for the event probably began, unconsciously, years ago when you first became aware of the impact spaces have on people. There are some places we come to that seem to speak to us. We feel we are at our best there; we walk a little taller and feel wittier, more attractive. To stage your wedding in one of your special places would be absolute heaven.

Unfortunately, many of our special places are not going to be available for the wedding. For me, the lobby of Radio City Music Hall, in the middle of New York City, has always had vast allure. I was introduced to the Music Hall when I was very young, and to me it represented glamour and all the wonderful adult things that are in short supply in a kid's life. But it's hardly the place to have a wedding, even though it does have a grand staircase!

▲▲▲▲▲▲▲

DETERMINING YOUR SPACE NEEDS

▼▼▼▼▼▼▼

By analyzing what the special places have to offer, you can establish some guidelines that will help you as you research locations. Spend a little time checking out your fantasies to zero in on the quality of the spaces that attract you. Long-gone department store Christmas windows are another of my personal favorites—I go for the glitter, the magic, every time.

My favorites tell me that I really like sparkle, dramatic, high-contrast lighting effects, and a pervasive theatricality. And while I certainly wouldn't want to duplicate a store window or the Music Hall, I can look for a space that will allow me to design and set up a decor that can give me some sparkle, some dramatic lighting effects, and a fairy-tale environment.

Both of you will have input into the space requirements for your wedding celebration, so begin by conjuring up a composite of your ideal space. Try to get it down to a few descriptive words, which will be easier to work with. Spend some time playing with this; you can create anything from an undersea kingdom to the Emerald City of Oz as long as you figure out exactly what you want.

If you agree, for example, on a woodsy, forest setting or a blossom-bedecked garden, fine. Both are do-able, even indoors in the middle of winter. Walls can be covered with greenery, garlands of flowers (real or fantasy) can outline entrances and exits, and floral scents can perfume the air.

Use your workbook Concept sheet to help guide and organize your ideas.

A more pragmatic consideration to be dealt with is how much space you need for the amount of people you are planning to invite. If the size of the space doesn't relate to the number of guests, you're in for trouble: A huge room, sparsely populated, somehow gives the impression that many guests didn't show up. Conversely, a tiny room crammed with people is unpleasant and makes for a very brief party.

If you are looking at indoor rental space, by all means check the local fire code. Public buildings generally have the legal occupancy limit posted prominently. The fire laws will tell you how many people legally can occupy the space. If the information is not posted someplace in the building, ask the rental agent. And take it seriously, please. "Occupancy by 150 people" means exactly that—no matter how many extra guests just happen to drop in.

Most of the estimates are based on the square footage of usable space available. Measure the width and length of the space, multiply them, and the answer is the square footage. For example, if the hall you are considering measures 40 feet by 50 feet, you have 2,000 square feet of potential party space. This also applies to outdoor space. If your backyard is 40 feet by 50 feet, you have 2,000 square feet to work with. The following space guidelines are useful:

For a stand-up cocktail reception, 6 to 7 square feet per person is advisable.

For a sit-down or buffet reception, 11 to 12 square feet per person is advisable.

LOCATIONS

Next, to accurately assess the usability of the space available, you have to subtract the floor space that will be taken up by tables and chairs, bar setups, dance floor, buffet tables, and so forth.

Table Sizes: These are rather standard, whether you rent or borrow them:

Size	*Seats*
Bridge table or 36-inch round table	4
Rectangular tables:	
4 feet by 30 inches	4 to 6
5 feet by 30 inches	6 to 8
6 feet by 30 inches	8 to 10
8 feet by 30 inches	10 to 12
Round tables:	
39-inch diameter	5
42-inch diameter	6
48-inch diameter	8
54-inch diameter	8 to 10
60-inch diameter	10
66-inch diameter	10 to 12
72-inch diameter	12
Oval tables:	
5 feet by 36 inches	8
6 feet by 36 inches	10
6 feet by 48 inches	12
7½ feet by 54 inches	14

Rental bars are generally available in 2½ feet, 4 feet, and 6 feet widths. The optimum service bar size is 6 feet. Allow a clear space of 6 feet around a service bar with a bartender and clear space of 9 feet to 10 feet around a self-service bar.

Rental Coatracks: Wintertime parties require either a coatroom or coatracks. Racks can be rented in 5-feet- or 6-feet-long sizes, which accommodate from thirty to fifty winter coats. In your space planning, leave several feet of space around each coatrack for winter boots, umbrellas, and carrying bags. Most rental coatracks have an upper shelf for hats.

Tents: This is a festive way to present an outdoor wedding party if you have access to cleared, level land. Most medium-sized communities have a tent and party equipment rental company that will deliver and erect a tent even to outlying rural areas. Check the classified section of your phone directory.

The more rural, the more complicated a tent party becomes, unfortunately, since you will want to be able to run electric lines to the tent and have some sort of bathroom facilities for the guests. Portable generators and outdoor toilets are rentable, of course, but every additional item increases the cost of the party. Still, it's hard to beat a tent for built-in gaiety.

While tents are wonderful, permits may be required in certain municipalities, and they are expensive to rent. Prices vary across the country, but you can expect to add from $5.00 to $10.00 per person onto your party budget. Check the rental company concerning the legalities, and also ask about their insurance coverage in case anything happens to the tent.

If you do go for a rental tent, be sure the contract you sign assures you that the rental company erects, maintains, and removes the tent. I'm pretty fearless about do-it-yourself jobs, but even I draw the line at party tents. While researching this book I heard tent-falling-down tales from coast to coast, and always after the food had been set out. . . .

An alternative to tent rentals is canopies or tent flies borrowed from camping

Tent flies can look marvelously festive

friends, purchased, or rented from a local camping equipment store. Canopies come with their own poles, generally 8 feet high, while flies are simply large rectangles of waterproof material with grommets set into the four edges. Flies can be suspended from trees or poles by running lines through the grommets and lashing the material in place. They are easy to set up and work well as temporary shelter.

If you live in a sunny part of the country, a pretty, alternate version of a fly can be made by sewing brightly colored fabrics together to cover the area you want for the party and adding loops onto the upper corners to accommodate the lashing lines. The fly can then be decorated with paint, appliqués, fringes, banners, and so forth. Secure them to trees or off the side of a building. They will not be waterproof but will look marvelous and create a festive party area with relatively little effort and expense.

Also, the handmade, decorated fly works fabulously as an open-sided cover over smaller areas such as the food service space, the bar, or the dance floor. Use them singly or in sets to create an outdoor cafe effect, turning your backyard or field into a quaint village square.

Guidelines to follow when figuring the size of the tent, fly, or canopy you will need are:

Number of People	Size Needed
60	20 feet by 30 feet
80	20 feet by 40 feet
125	30 feet by 40 feet
150	30 feet by 50 feet
200	30 feet by 70 feet
250	40 feet by 60 feet
300	40 feet by 80 feet

Making a Dance Floor

1. *Lay out eight sheets of 4' × 8' plywood.*

2. *Join them lengthwise by butting the edges together and screwing long 1" × 3" boards over the junctures—#1 and #5 are joined with #2 and #6; then #2 and #6 are joined with #3 and #7, etc. All eight sheets should end up being joined into one large wood slab.*

3. *After the plywood sheets have been joined together, add small lengths (cut to fit) of 1" × 3" boards between the long 1" × 3" boards, to serve as cross braces.*

Most wedding receptions include dancing, so provisions for a dance floor have to be made when planning an outdoor wedding party. Tent rental companies offer dance floors, often in a rental package along with the tent. Dance floors usually come in 4-feet-by-8-feet sections of finished plywood installed over a low wooden framework placed on the ground. Again, they are rather expensive and can be constructed easily at home if anybody has a need for post-wedding plywood sheets.

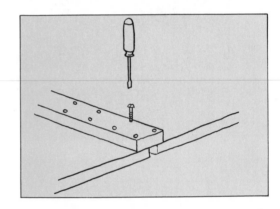

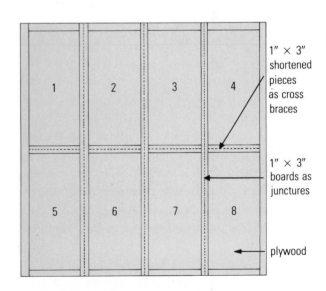

1" × 3" shortened pieces as cross braces

1" × 3" boards as junctures

plywood

Wooden dance floor, made from eight sheets of plywood, seen from underneath

LOCATIONS

▲▲▲▲▲▲▲▲

FINDING THE PERFECT LOCATION

▼▼▼▼▼▼▼

Having pulled together your space needs, you are now ready to go out and research locales to see what's available. Use the following as a checklist when you are shopping. The bare bones requirements for acceptable party places include the following:

- Sufficient square footage for your guest list
- Adequate electric power to bring in extra sound, lighting, and kitchen equipment
- Adequate kitchen facilities or adjacent areas to set up food and beverage service areas
- Enough bathrooms for the number of guests
- Parking space to accommodate guests' cars
- Heat and/or air conditioning if needed
- Space for coat storage
- Dance floor if desired
- Some provision for trash pickup after the event
- Access to the space twenty-four hours prior to the wedding

If you have lived in your area for even a few years, you probably know the usual places that your neighbors use for weddings and other special occasions. Most hotels and restaurants have party rooms. Private clubs and halls attached to churches and temples often stay solvent through rentals. Fraternal organizations, unions, schools, and corporations some-

There is a reference book used by many film and video people entitled *Places*. Each copy contains five regional sections that list specific locations that can be rented in New England, Mid Atlantic states, New York City, the South, Midwest, and West. *Places* is published every two years by Tenth House Enterprises, 244 East 86th Street, New York, NY 10028. The book is available only by mail order, and the cover price of $18.95 includes a novel telephone location hot line service. If you cannot find a space you want through the printed listings, you may call and ask for additional data and/or help on special project needs. For further information about *Places* call 212–737–7536.

times rent out space, as do local governments, museums, and historical sites. Parks and botanical gardens generally have picturesque spots available. Chambers of commerce, departments of tourism, and historical societies are worth checking for unusual sites, as are municipal ferryboat, beach, and park commissions.

The main question with all of the above is whether or not you can do your own catering, sound, and decorating. If you are forced to use the organization's in-house services, there will be a markup on each item purchased, plus a labor charge that might well destroy your budget. If money is a consideration, what you are seeking is merely a bare space that you can bring your party into.

Begin your location research as soon as you set the wedding date. Good places get booked months in advance. Photographers and film companies are always on the lookout for terrific locations. If your city is large enough to have a municipal office that coordinates filming, call and ask for

L O C A T I O N S

LOCATIONS

reference material on available locations. If there are film companies in your community, call them and ask if they have a location finder whom they could recommend to you. A brief conference with a professional location finder might save you a great deal of time and effort.

▲▲▲▲▲▲▲

CREATING A FLOOR PLAN

▽▽▽▽▽▽▽

Once you have selected your space, it is time to do a scale floor plan to see just how it will work. If you have rented

space, ask the rental agent for a copy of the floor plan. If none exists, you will have to draw one up yourselves. This might seem like a lot of extra effort, but without it you have no real assurance that your party plans will actually function in the space you have selected.

To do the floor plan you'll need access to the party space—enough time to measure all the way around the entire room. Measuring floor space is tedious when done by one person, so both of you should do it or find a friend who will hold the other end of the tape and help record the measurements.

Once you've arranged for access, you'll need the page of graph paper on page 201

Sample floor plan

*All lights have four 40-watt bulbs

X—double electric sockets

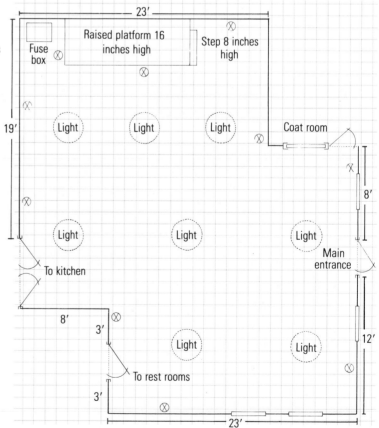

in the workbook section, a large metal tape measure, some ordinary lead pencils, and several pencils of different colors.

By using graph paper you can condense space measurements, so a large area can be worked with on one page. Establish a scale to work in by deciding what amount of space each square on the graph paper represents. Usually one square can represent 1 foot of space. If your space is exceptionally large, however, you may want to decide that one square equals 2 feet of measured space. To decide, pace off your space, count the squares on the graph paper, and see what will fit best for your needs.

Once you've established your scale, begin measuring the space. A good starting place is right at the entrance. Lay the tape measure along one of the walls, count how many feet of unbroken space there are, and draw a pencil line on the graph paper corresponding to the number of squares. That is, for 10 feet of space, make your line ten squares long. Continue measuring all around the space, filling in your graph paper until you have an accurate outline of the entire area. Be sure to indicate all windows, doors, platforms, pillars, stairs, closets, fireplaces, and radiators, since these will affect the placement of your tables and service areas.

With the colored pencils indicate the electric fuse or switch box, outlets, and existing lighting fixtures. Be specific on these, noting the number of bulbs in each fixture, the wattage used, and the power available in the electrical outlets. These will affect your decor and special effects. For outdoor locations use the colored pen-

cils to show how you will route power lines to the party area and what you plan to do about bathroom facilities.

If you plan to have the wedding ceremony take place in the same room as the reception, sketch out where the "altar" can be placed and designate the "aisle" that will lead you there and the placement of chairs. Be sure your aisle is wide enough to accommodate two people walking side by side, one of them wearing a fancy dress!

Doing the floor plan not only lets you see how the space will function, it helps you decide exactly what size tables, bars, and so forth, will best serve your needs. Use the standard measurements given earlier in this chapter for rental equipment, and be sure to measure the dimensions of everything you will be borrowing or bringing from home. Translate the measurements into the same scale you are using for the floor plan; for example, if you are using rectangular tables that measure 4 feet by 30 inches, you'll need to sketch in tables that are 4 squares by 2½ squares.

The more complete your floor plan, the more secure you can be about the operation of the event. By "seeing" on paper how the food will get from the preparation area to the tables or what routes guests will take to the bathroom, you can circumvent potential trouble spots. As you work with the other chapters of this book that pertain to the physical setting, you will be adding to your basic floor plan, penciling in lighting and sound equipment, and adding decorative elements.

Once you have the basic plan drawn up, make several photocopies of it so you can use one for your lighting plan, one for your sound system plan, some for food and beverage service, and a few to give to the friends who will help set up the party. And keep a copy of your floor plan with your work sheets. If everybody involved knows just about where everything is supposed to go, the setup will go faster and more smoothly.

▼ *The Location worksheets can be found on pages 200–201.*

LOCATIONS

6

▲▲▲▲▲▲▲

INVITATIONS
AND
ANNOUNCEMENTS

▼▼▼▼▼▼▼

▼▼▼▼▼▼▼

INVITATIONS AND ANNOUNCEMENTS

Spreading the news via announcements and invitations is the beginning of the excitement. They can be anything from the traditional multi-enveloped engraved packet to whatever pleases you. The choices are many, and the materials you ▼▼▼▼▼▼ have to work with are fantastic!

▲▲▲▲▲▲▲

THE GUEST LIST

▼▼▼▼▼▼▼

Begin by making a list of all the people to whom these will be sent so that you know the numbers you are dealing with. A mailing of five hundred or six hundred pieces will have to be more mass produced than a mailing of fifty or sixty. The smaller the list, the more personal and hand detailed each piece can be. (If you have already created a shower invitation list, use it as a base for the big event data.)

Once the overall list is compiled, you can divide it into groups:

1) people who will be invited to the ceremony and the reception; these will receive invitations to both;

2) people who will be invited only to the ceremony; these will not get an invitation to the reception;

3) people who will not be invited to attend any part of the celebration but whom you want to notify of the event; they will receive an announcement card, or a copy of the wedding invitation sent the day after the wedding.

Remember to get input from everybody concerned, in both families. Your grandmother's guest list is just as important to her as your mother's is to her. Weddings are strange, tribal events. For some reason people remember with awesome accuracy who was and who was not included at weddings that happened decades ago. Avoid hard feelings and double-check from the very beginning.

▲▲▲▲▲▲▲

CHOOSING A STYLE

▽▽▽▽▽▽▽

Next, do some research on wedding invitations. Visit your local printer, photocopy, or stationery store. You will be shown books of sample wedding announcements and invitations that you can order through them. You'll be amazed at the variety those books offer. If you have any doubts about the "correctness" of doing an offbeat invitation, one look at a

sample book will dispel your worries.

After seeing the samples and getting price quotes you may decide to go ahead and order them from the book. If so, get firm delivery dates for the printed matter and request the boxes of envelopes immediately. Then you can begin hand addressing them while the printing is being done, thereby spreading an arduous task over several weeks. Yes, wedding invitations and announcements are always hand addressed.

The invitations to the wedding and the reception must be mailed at least three to four weeks prior to the event. This allows your guests time to respond. Invitations to attend the ceremony may be mailed out two to three weeks in advance. Announcements should be mailed out the day after the wedding.

You may want to personalize traditional invitations ordered from a printer. Artist Jill Tannone transformed rather ordinary printed invitations by lightly spray painting a misty border of pastel colors around the message. The effect was lovely and very personal, and the time saved was gratefully put into other facets of the wedding celebration.

If you decide to do your own invitations or have an artistic friend or relative create them for you, begin by considering what feeling you want your invitations to convey. New York illustrator Richard Hernandez, whose work appears in major magazines, believes the wedding really starts with the invitations—they are the first material evidence of the ceremony.

Richard suggests that you "think about who you are and who the people are who will receive the invitations. How do you want them to feel about you and the cele-

INVITATIONS AND ANNOUNCEMENTS

bration? If you're yuppies, you'll probably want silver engraved all over. If you're hippies, you might send your invitations out in the form of beads. If you're in a motorcycle gang, you can have your invitations studded on black leather."

He continues in a more serious vein, "Think about it because there are always two avenues of communication in everything. There's the literal translation of the word, imparting the information, and then there's the subliminal message your audience is receiving. The literal translation will get your guests to the church on time, but the subliminal message will set the stage for your celebration."

New York graphic designer Naomi Berger echoed the Hernandez suggestion: "Let your invitations tell your audience very definite things about you and your wedding. Each detail you choose is important, from the paper stock, color, and typeface to the layout and more. You will be more successful when preparing your invitations if you approach the project in the same way as a professional designing an ad. It all comes down to zeroing in on the total story that you want to convey."

Return to the conceptualization workbook page where you put together some word descriptions of your special places to help you select the perfect party space. Try out those same words again for your invitations. They will point you in the direction of invitations and announcements that accurately reflect the tone of the celebration. My words, "glitter" and "dramatic/theatrical," certainly steer me away from plain white paper with black printing!

Relate your words to colors and to shapes; even scents can be included if you wish. A flowery, garden feeling might include a pressed flower photocopied onto pastel, scented paper, or a few paper rose petals folded into the announcement may flutter out when the envelope is opened, or an interesting folded paper origami flower may bear your message when the paper is unfolded.

Richard gave us a few examples of creative designing: A photographer friend had a party invitation set up in ordinary type on plain white paper. Then he photographed the invitation, had slides made up of the photograph, and mailed them out. His guests received these interesting little packages that were very secretive. They would open the box to find a little slide that they had to hold up to the light and squint at in order to read the party invitation. Once they deciphered the message his guests were delighted—and the anticipation for the event far exceeded any that an ordinary note would create.

Another friend, an art director, created his own Christmas cards by obtaining a pattern from a children's craft book showing how to fold paper to form a cube. He incorporated a small hole into the pattern, and bought a quantity of plastic snow. The art director silk-screened a sky, fluffy clouds, and his message onto stiff paper. Then he folded each sheet into the cube shape and added some snow during the folding. As the recipient turned the cube to read the Christmas greeting, snow drifted down from the hole!

In other words, you don't have to stick to the ordinary when you design your invitations. As long as both the literal message and the subliminal message come through loud and clear, your invitations will be fine.

Let's talk literal message. If you want to use the traditional wording, it goes like this:

Mr. and Mrs. George F. Hunt, Jr.
request the honour of your presence
at the marriage of their daughter
Amy Munson Hunt
to
George Wayne Sakers
Saturday, the eighth of October
at twelve o'clock noon
Saint Francis Church
Old Long Ridge Road
Stamford, Connecticut

The reception invitation is on a separate card that is enclosed in the folded traditional invitation. The wording can vary from the flowery, "The pleasure of your company is requested at a . . ." to a simpler statement:

Luncheon
immediately following the ceremony
Old Mill Lane
Stamford, Connecticut

An R.S.V.P. card with a stamped, addressed envelope is also often included, making it as easy as possible for everybody to reply. It is an extra expense, but the peace of mind you'll get from knowing who is coming is worth it! Across the top, the reply card might say:

The favor of a reply is requested
by September 25, 1988

The lower two-thirds of the card is blank so the invitees may write their acceptances or regrets.

When preparing your own invitations, some or all of the above wording may be incorporated, or you can work out your own phrases. Anything goes, as long as you include all the facts:

Who (persons sending out the invitation)
What (are inviting the reader to a wedding)
Why (because two people want to be legally wed)
Where (location)
When (date and time)
How (operationally—the ceremony will be at x place, the reception will be at x place, and please respond by a certain date)

By the time you've established your wording you probably will have some ideas about the execution of the invitation.

If folded paper interests you, there are great patterns in origami books and paper craft books. Pop-up books found in the children's section of bookstores are delightful and can be copied so that a section of paper pops up when the invitation is unfolded. Just buy a copy of the pop-up book you like, carefully separate the pop-up page elements, noting where they are folded and glued together, duplicate the folds, and glue in your own materials.

Perhaps you want some artwork on your invitation. Richard Hernandez tells us, "Many people are hesitant about artwork because they don't know how to think about it—but art is all around us. It could be a rubbing of a bit of lace or a simple collage that you photocopy, something that imparts some of the feeling you are trying to express. It could be anything graphic that reproduces well enough to get your idea across."

If you or a friend can do beautiful art-

INVITATIONS AND ANNOUNCEMENTS

The Pictorial Archive Series by Dover Publications is probably the best known set of clip books. They are inexpensive paperbound books and well worth checking. You simply get the Dover book of your choice, photocopy the art you like, and use it as part of the "paste-up" or "mechanical" that readies your invitation for reproduction. If nobody near you carries the Dover line, write to their home office and request a mail-order catalog so you can order directly:

Dover Publications, Inc.
31 East 2nd Street
Mineola, NY 11501-3582

If you want a good introduction to the mysteries of the rubber stamp world, locate a copy of *The Rubber Stamp Album,* written by Miller & Thompson and published by Workman Publishing Company. If your local library doesn't have a copy, you can order it from the publisher. Send $6.95 (the cover price) plus $1.00 for postage and handling to:

Workman Publishing Company
1 West 39th Street
New York, NY 10018

An outstanding group of fine art stamps are available from a company called Portfolio Rubber Stamps. The Portfolio line is a far cry from the quaint old-fashioned stamp art found in most rubber stamp stores. The drawings are done by two recognized artists, Maud Guilfoyle and Peregrine Higgins. The graceful lines and elegant detail make the Portfolio stamps ideal for wedding use; many lovely invitations have utilized them.

For a Portfolio Rubber Stamps catalog send $2.00 to:

Portfolio Rubber Stamps
11 Roosevelt Avenue
Westwood, NJ 07675
The $2.00 is refundable with first purchase.

work, especially pen-and-ink drawings, you are home free. If not, you need to locate art that feels right to you and will reproduce well. The legality of using somebody else's art and not paying a royalty fee does not enter in since you are doing invitations to a private affair. As long as you restrict the "borrowed" art to your own personal use you are within the law.

A fun wedding invitation I received a few years ago used a cartoon from the *New Yorker* magazine showing a very cool, hip couple in full 1960s regalia clinking glasses at a crowded cocktail party. The caption read, "Right time. Right place." The artwork was loose and sketchy, and inside, the message was done in calligraphy that carried out the feeling of the cartoon figures. Anyone opening this invitation knew the wedding celebration was going to be nontraditional, inventive, a great party done with a rollicking sense of humor.

Bookstores, art supply stores, and libraries have copies of source books published to service professional artists. Called "clip books," they contain a vast variety of artwork including banners, borders, and signs that are in the public domain and thus may be used in print without paying royalties. Much of the material is old; for example, wonderful Victorian floral borders and traditional decorative elements, which work well for wedding announcements.

Another approach to using published art is to change it slightly, adding your own personal touch; for example, you might find a news photo of a royal wedding and change it by replacing Charles's and Diana's or Andrew's and Fergie's heads with snapshots of each of you. The cut-and-paste technique opens a myriad of possibilities! Any funny pictures, old movie stills, circus posters, or cartoons can be doctored to represent the two of you. Photocopiers or your local camera store can help you in reducing or blowing up material to get the size you want. Be sure to do your glueing with rubber cement, and carefully clean up any excess cement that seeps out the sides.

Rubber stamps have come into their own as a wonderful source of art. You can have a stamp made up from your own artwork by any of the rubber stamp companies listed in the Yellow Pages; or you can purchase some incredibly beautiful fine art rubber stamps; or you can carve a stamp of your own out of an eraser. Inked stamp pads are available in every color of the rainbow, including some multicolor pads.

Peregrine Higgins offers advice to those wanting to carve their own stamps: "People who do a lot of carving become passionate about favorite eraser brands. The Green Jumbo by Eberhard Faber and the Staedtler Mars Plastic Grand White are considered the most desirable. Avoid spongy, gummy erasers. They're difficult to carve and won't hold up to a sharp impression."

You'll need X-Acto knives or small scalpels plus an inexpensive set of linoleum block carving tools. The tools come four or five to a box and are available in art supply and craft supply stores.

Begin by drawing or tracing your design on paper with a soft black lead pencil. Place the paper on the eraser and carefully transfer by drawing heavily on the back of the paper. This means the

drawing will be reversed, which you will have cleverly allowed for, especially if you are doing letters. For a first-time project we recommend you choose a simple shape such as a heart or a star.

Draw the design again with a soft pencil and go over it with a black ink pen. Avoid ballpoint pens since they tend to dig into the eraser. Now you're ready to cut.

Always cut away from your design at a definite angle. This provides the stability for a clear impression. Never undercut!

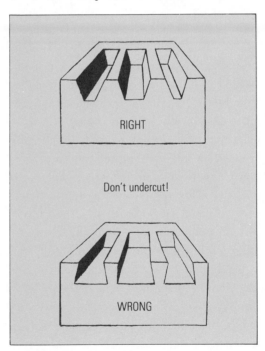

Rubber stamps cut from an eraser

Cut only a millimeter at a time, carving the surplus away by degrees. Use the gouge from the linoleum set to remove surplus rubber from large areas. Make sample prints as you go along so that you can revise the cutting if necessary. To duplicate, print your new stamp directly onto another eraser and cut out as before.

A fun addition to the rubber stamps is an embossing powder available from rubber stamp shops or by direct mail. The powder is sprinkled on a freshly stamped image, clinging to the wet ink. After the excess powder is shaken off, the paper is held above the soleplate of a hot iron. The heat from the iron melts the powder, leaving a raised, embossed-like impression. The embossing powder also works with watercolors or any water-based inks.

Calligraphy is another good technique for wedding invitations. Again, check local phone books, art schools, and/or party shops to locate professional calligraphers. The owners of Portfolio Rubber Stamps, Peregrine and Maud, are both skilled calligraphers who heartily recommend trying it yourself for home-produced invitations. You have to come up with only one perfect copy of each letter, and the letters are then pasted up into sentences to form your message; that copy can be easily reproduced as many times as your guest list requires. In other words, you don't have to slave away hand lettering each invitation unless you want to.

Calligraphy pen sets and instruction books are sold in most art supply and stationery stores. The rudiments are not difficult to learn, but like most hand skills, calligraphy needs a few serious hours of practice in order to turn out acceptable script.

Use checked graph paper with pale blue lines or the lined paper that comes with Pentalic and other brand-name pen sets. Take plenty of time with each letter or try tracing letters from somebody else's calligraphy alphabet onto graph paper. Cut and paste is the good technique here, so focus on getting a group of letters or

words good enough to clip out and assemble into a "mechanical" for reproduction.

Peregrine suggests you pay attention to the spacing of letters; do it by eye rather than by checks on the graph paper. When a word looks good to you, use it. Everybody is exposed to printed messages all the time. Trust your eye to have picked up a subliminal opinion about spacing, and don't worry about infinitesimally small measurements.

Try to make your calligraphy easy to read. If you find you work more easily doing large letters and words, no problem. After you assemble the text, pasted up as your mechanical, then take it to a photostat or photocopy house and have it mechanically reduced to whatever size you actually want your invitation to be. The tools of the professional are extremely useful and are yours for the asking.

The Portfolio owners combine calligraphy with art rubber stamps to obtain terrific effects. A flutter of flowers and a spill of hearts twining around the message can be stunning. Using different colored ink pads for the rubber stamps adds another dimension to your invitation, as does duplicating and masking out images to create new patterns. The stamps can be put on before or after the calligraphy is reproduced, giving you a choice of doing each invitation as a piece of original art or having the entire amount reproduced for you. Be lavish with the use of your stamps—more is better in this case!

Silk screening your invitations is another possibility, if you know somebody skilled in the craft. Making a set of screens is an exacting job. Many art schools and craft centers offer silk screening classes, however, so you might

Wedding invitation—calligraphy with rubber stamps

come across somebody who will do it for you.

▲▲▲▲▲▲▲▲

SELECTING TYPE

▽▽▽▽▽▽▽

For the text, a product called transfer or press type is most commonly used. Art supply stores have catalogs from the Presstype and Chartpack companies and other suppliers. Press type comes on a transparent sheet and consists of sets of letters, upper and lower case, that you transfer onto paper by rubbing the underside of the sheet with a metal object such

as a coin. Complete "how-to" directions come with each sheet.

Press type is inexpensive, about six or seven dollars a sheet. Probably one sheet will be enough to fill your needs. Write out the complete message on scrap paper so you can plan how you're going to place the sentences. Using the graph paper as a guide, transfer the press type letters, working letter by letter to form sentences. Do each sentence individually, clip them out, and align the strips on a larger piece of paper. You can have them "justified left," which means lined up flush left, or justified right if you want. The grid on your graph paper will help you with placement.

Borders and designs are also available in press type. There are colored, shaded, open, and pseudo-calligraphy type, and many more. Richard Hernandez echoes Peregrine Higgins' caution: "Putting type together is not easy. You've got to do it by eye. Push the letters tightly against each other so they look well designed. Do not rely on the graph paper's spacing for measurements. Trust your intuition and sensibilities."

Naomi Berger suggests that you have your type set by a printer and then do your own mechanical. You'll save a lot of time, and she feels the money you'll save by using transfer type is not that much. Typographers' prices vary, so get several estimates from local printers. Write out your message in order to know exactly how you want each sentence to read; show it to the printer and ask to see what type faces the printer carries. You will have a good selection of type: from the common newspaperlike faces to exotic, special event types. Select one that pleases you, and place your order.

The printer will give you a long sheet or two of paper with the sentences printed out, but not necessarily in any order. When you make your mechanical you will scissor out the sentences and glue them in place, justified right or left, and so forth.

You will need the following:

Bristol board or any other stiff paper
Rubber cement
T square and triangle
Exacto knife and sharp scissors
Sharpened fine point pencils
New bottle of white correction fluid, the kind used for correcting typewriter errors
Very clean, dry hands

Naomi takes us through the mechanical-making steps:

1) Using the T square for accuracy, draw faint pencil lines indicating the outer dimensions of the invitation, card, and so on.

2) With the same equipment, rule in faint horizontal pencil lines indicating the placement of the lines of type—either your own press type version, calligraphy, or type from the local printer.

3) Perch the triangle on the upper edge of the square and faintly rule in a vertical line indicating the right or left, justifying or centering.

4) You have in front of you the lines of type or lettering you've done plus any decorative elements. Place each element onto the paper, arranging everything so you can see how the finished product is going to look. Take your time with this step; this is where your "eye" comes in.

5) When you arrive at a placement you like, you're ready to begin glueing. Put the first line of type, neatly trimmed, face down on scrap paper, coat the back lightly with rubber cement, and place it on the first horizontal pencil line. The rubber cement, used in a single application, allows you to pick it up and replace it any number of times until you are happy with it.

6) Continue on down the page until you get the total message glued down. Set it aside to dry while you paste up the reception cards, announcement (if different from the invitation), and any other enclosures.

7) That's it! Tape a protective sheet over the finished mechanicals so the type face won't get dirty or disturbed on its way to the photocopy shop.

INVITATIONS AND ANNOUNCEMENTS

The mechanicals can be done as much in advance as you like. Keep them in a safe, dry place while you shop for wonderful paper stock. If there is a paper store in your area, check there first for interesting paper and envelopes. Printers and copy shops rarely have anything other than the most mundane stock, suitable for business reports and little else. Shop around and locate the weight and color that goes with your wedding. Consider wrapping papers, book endpapers, rice papers, or other nontraditional materials if they fit into your image of your wedding. Envelopes do not have to match except for the classic, traditional invitations.

When you're ready to have the mechanicals duplicated, take them to the photocopy shop in your area that does the cleanest, best work. Do not use a home or small office copier; you need the big, state-of-the-art machines that give a fine reproduction that looks like printing. Remember to take your bottle of correction fluid with you.

Show the mechanicals to the copy people and ask them to run off a duplicate of each mechanical. The pages you get back will show the cut edge lines from everything you pasted down; it will look dreadful. Use the correction fluid to white out everything on the duplicate that you don't want to show on the finished product. It's tedious work and is best done slowly. When you think you've got it all covered up, ask the copy shop people to run off another duplicate and show it to you.

Keep doing this until the duplicate comes out looking perfect. Several run-throughs are usually needed. Always work off the first copy, correcting and recorrecting. When you're satisfied, give the copy people the wonderful paper stock you've purchased and have them run off the necessary number. Your invitations will be unique and will truly set the stage for the celebration that is to come.

▼ *The Invitations worksheet can be found on pages 204–5.*

▲▲▲▲▲▲▲

COSTUMES

▼▼▼▼▼▼▼

7

COSTUMES

For today's bride, "something old, something new, something borrowed, something blue" comes down to choosing absolutely anything you like for your wedding costumes. Women's Wear Daily, *the bible of the garment industry, backed up this theory* ▼ ▼ ▼ ▼ ▼ ▼ *in a recent wedding roundup, saying that although the traditional look is "in," every look is acceptable today. Individual preference is the name of the game.*

The need for research probably doesn't merit mentioning. Most newly engaged couples race out and scoop up copies of all the bride's magazines. Then they sit, glassy-eyed, surrounded by mountains of ornate photos, advice on everything from silver patterns to contraception, and lavish color page spreads touting choice spots to go for the honeymoon.

You can avoid all the confusion and save yourselves time by referring to your conceptualization workbook sheet. You visualized a certain kind of look for your wedding: formal, informal, day, evening, traditional, country, modern, and so forth. What were all those people wearing in your visualization? Long gowns, short dresses, tuxedos, business suits? And, most important, what were the colors?

Erudite books have been written, courses have been taught, and lectures have been given about color; it is too vast a topic to examine thoroughly here. Let it suffice to say we all have favorite colors. Logically, you can use some of your favorite colors for your wedding, selecting those shades and tints that fit into your overall concept. For example, black, white, silver, and a touch of vermilion will give you a high-contrast, trendy, dramatic color scheme. On the other hand, muted shades of pink, rose, and lavender, or of yellow, peach, and apricot, will give you a soft, pretty, almost dreamy color scheme.

If "your" color scheme doesn't surface easily and beyond a doubt, use the fashion and home decorating magazines to show you how different colors and shades go together. Sofas, pillows, and draperies might seem far away from wedding costumes, but the color messages come through just as clearly as with scarves, jackets, and handbags. And don't be afraid of offbeat color schemes. If you come up with a combination that you like, then use it. There are no hard-and-fast rules today.

Once you've reconstructed your visuals you'll know what general look you're after. Then photocopy the Costume Worksheet pages, and you're ready to decide how you are going to acquire the costumes.

You can buy, borrow, rent, make, or combine any or all of these.

If you have to buy everything, you are at the mercy of the local stores, with your choices limited to whatever they happen to have in stock. Also, buying retail is the most expensive way to costume a wedding, so explore all alternatives. Sometimes a combination of sewing and buying works; beautiful store-bought blouses may be paired with simple long skirts sewn from a fabulous fabric.

Renting wedding clothes works best for the men in the party. Unfortunately, a men's dress suit rental is expensive, averaging between forty and eighty dollars for a wedding. Generally, however, it covers everything the man will need: tie, cummerbund, and so forth. Wedding dress rentals are available, usually in larger cities or from mail-order costume houses, but are rarely wonderful. Unless you can handpick a rental and have it fitted on you, the bridal gown is best gotten from other sources.

Borrowing is a good possibility for the groomsmen. Despite the vast variations shown in the bridal magazines, a tuxedo is still a tuxedo. If it fits, it looks great! Borrowing a wedding gown or using a family gown is a fine idea only if it's a dress you really adore. Don't get talked into anything you are not truly enthusiastic about, especially for your one and only wedding.

New York designer and fashion consultant June Francis spoke to that point when she talked with us about weddings: "Certain things must be clarified before any real clothes planning can be done. I mean, you have to sort out who is in charge, who has the final, ultimate say in all questions. In many cases, I think the bride is too acquiescent to the parents' wishes when it's really not the parents' wedding. You, the couple, have to decide

C O S T U M E S

67

COSTUMES

what you want and proceed from there. However, you also have to have parents who can relinquish control over what you want. It's your wedding. Get the control question out of the way in the very beginning, scary though it may be."

If home sewing is available to you, June suggests you approach making the costumes the same way a professional designer does a line of clothes. You begin by making "color boards," that is, assembling a collage of fabrics you like. First, shop all the piece goods stores and get swatches of the fabric possibilities that are in your color scheme. Then take sheets of stiff notebook-size paper and pin up the swatches, arranged in an order that is pleasing to you. Hang the collages up in some highly visible spot for several days to see how each grouping lives together. By the end of the week you'll know, beyond any doubt, which combination you want for your wedding. Keep going until you come up with boards you really love, and you've solved your color and fabric questions!

The final color board has lots of other uses. It's invaluable for selling the attendants and the mothers on your color scheme, adding exciting reality to your bridesmaids' luncheon meeting. Also, the board should accompany you on shopping trips for almost everything: flowers, trimmings, accessories, even the table linens that have to be keyed to your colors to give unity to the entire production.

Explore the possibilities of pretty prints for the attendants' dresses. "Roses are big news in today's fabric market," says June Francis. "For a fresh look consider the honor attendants in solid rose color and the maids in cabbage rose prints that pick

Shopping for fabrics must be governed to a certain extent by the skill of your sewing volunteers. Don't expect them to handle chiffon, a most difficult fabric, if they've had most of their successes with cottons and woolens. Pile fabrics, such as rayon velvets, are also tricky for home sewers; velveteen is a better choice since it has more dimensional stability.

up the honor attendants' colors. The theme could be carried into the flowers, the flower girl's outfit, the boutonnieres, and so forth."

Most of the large pattern book companies have a small section of wedding gowns and attendants' dresses; some even have patterns for men's ties, ascots, and cummerbunds. Be sure to check the women's dress, evening wear, and lingerie sections as well. Almost any garment can be converted into suitable wedding wear through choice of fabric, decorations, change of hemline, and other minor pattern adjustments.

Select a sewing pattern for the bridal gown first and then pick a similar style for the attendants. Keep fullness and hemlines identical for visual unity. If your gown will be floor length and full skirted, the attendants' should be the same. Again, work for visual unity. A word of caution: Schedule the final dress fittings no more than three days before the wedding. Attendants are prone to going on last-minute crash diets so they'll look as sleek as possible, and it can wreak havoc on the fit.

Pay attention to the undergarments everybody will need for the gowns. If a skirt must spread in a graceful A-line, something has to hold out the hemline. Lack of proper undergarments can ruin a wonderful dress, making it look limp and skimpy. Floor-length petticoats are usually the answer, and you can add layers of ruffles from the knee down to create the right flare.

The pattern pieces for the skirt usually can be used for the undergarment. The fabric can be any inexpensive muslin or stiff synthetic if it is color-matched to the outer fabric. Even the heaviest outer fabric will be affected by contrasting lingerie, so don't take a chance.

New York costume designer K. L. (Kathy) Fredericks, whose work is seen on television and in the theater, recommends looking into specialty patterns available by mail order if you aren't enchanted with what the big companies are offering in their catalogs. She suggests checking the following sources:

Past Patterns
2017 Eastern, S.E.
Grand Rapids, MI 49507
Telephone: 616-245-9456
They have a catalog of patterns from 1830 to 1939.

Cobble Classics
P. O. Box 206
Ashley Falls, MA 01222
They have patterns for sleeves, bodices, skirts, and so forth, all interchangeable.

Ethnic Assessories
Box 250
Forestville, CA 95436
Folkwear patterns.

Kathy's theatrical costumes are ornate and highly decorated. She and her staff rely on seed pearls, sequins, lace appliqués, beaded patches, and the like, glued onto the basic garments. This is an ideal way to transform very simple garments, either new or old, into fabulous creations. She uses a commercial adhesive called

bridal cement, which dries clear so it can be used on the face of any fabric. Happily, a similar consumer product is available under the brand name *Sobo* and is stocked by most craft supply stores.

Kathy's glueing technique is as follows:

Place layers of white tissue paper under the garment. Stretch the garment taut, weighting it with heavy objects. Work with a motif or decorative pattern sketched out in front of you for easy reference. Since clothing is generally soft and moves on the body, the pattern need not be followed slavishly; just get the general idea. If you haven't thought out a pattern, place the pearls, appliqués, and so forth on the garment and play with them until you come up with a placement you like. Remember, more is better when fancying up a dress, so be lavish with the seed pearls!

Dot the garment with glue, pick up the individual elements with a tweezer, and set them in place. Work section by section, allowing plenty of drying time before you move the garment around. A certain amount will always fall off after the first glueing, so begin this project enough in advance so you can reglue at leisure.

You might want to reconstruct an antique dress for the bridal gown or seriously alter a family heirloom to fit properly. Victorian and Edwardian dresses are immensely popular now; they have great charm and can be found at antique clothing shops and flea markets that cater to collectors.

When we were planning Catherine and Greg's wedding, the bridal gown was the one thing we didn't need to search for. Cath has been a flea market addict all her life, and on a shopping expedition in her

COSTUMES

teen years she brought home a tattered Edwardian afternoon dress. The garment, of yellowing linen and lace, looked rather ratty, but she washed it by hand and then tucked it away in the back of the sewing area, where it remained for some years. When the time came for the wedding, she pulled it out, dusty and wrinkled, and announced that this was it as far as she was concerned.

The man at the dry cleaning store couldn't believe we were serious when we brought it in. "It's in shreds," he announced. "I can't do anything with that. At least sew it together some more. Then I'll try." So we began to rebuild the dress, working from the inside, lining it with strong sheer nylon and then tacking the shredded linen onto the nylon.

The dress had had satin rosettes outlining the bodice. Many were missing, but we were able to reconstruct them by carefully taking apart one of the originals and following the fold lines until we could produce some look-alikes. Many of the lace insets were also beyond repair, so we had to duplicate them in the same way. The high lace collar had totally decomposed, leaving nothing to even copy, but Catherine suggested we scrap that and go for a plain round neck bound by lace, which was easily accomplished. At the wedding she wore a cameo that had belonged to her grandmother, pinned to the center of the neckline, and the original high collar wasn't missed a bit.

All in all, Catherine's flea market dress turned out to be beautiful and added charm to the event that we would not have achieved with a brand new wedding gown. The authentic period costume look of it proved to be the jumping-off place for the

style of the attendants' dresses—it was a lavender and lace wedding, enjoyed by everyone.

Shop carefully if you want to buy an heirloom dress. Very few are ever in wearable condition, but repairs as we did for Catherine can be done by anyone with modest sewing skills. Often the bodice and underarm areas are damaged and need repair. If, after dry cleaning, the fabric is sturdy enough to stand heat, try applying iron-on interfacing to the underside. Use a lightweight facing and work in small areas, overlapping the facing if necessary.

If heat doesn't seem to be a good idea, you will have to rebuild the bodice from underneath using sturdy, color-matched sheer nylon or a fine cotton batiste. If you have access to a dress form, put the garment on it inside out, pin pieces of the nylon to cover the worn places, and then hand stitch them in place. Reinforce with many little stitches, catching up the surrounding areas for extra strength.

If no dress form is available, turn the dress inside out, roll towels around books or shoe boxes, and slip them inside to hold the dress in a somewhat rounded shape. Slide a magazine between towel and dress so you have a slick surface to work against. Then proceed as above.

To enlarge an antique dress or to replace absolutely shredded sections, locate plain white fabric that closely resembles the rest of the garment; that is, use satin for satin, linen for linen. Avoid using synthetics since you'll have to color-match, and many synthetics are difficult to dye at home.

Cut strips of the replacement fabric and pin them in place. To enlarge, open the side seams and add strips; pin them in until a fit can be achieved. When you get the fit you like, hand sew or machine sew the strips in place.

Antique dresses usually have discolored into yellowy beige so you have to dye the strips to match the authentic parts of the garment before you sew them in place. We had to tint the lace and satin we used to repair Catherine's dress. Do the coloring with strong tea or coffee rather than using commercial fabric dyes. Soak scraps, then dry and press them, experimenting until you get an acceptable color match. Watercolor paint sets can also be used to color small fabric inserts. The permanence of the dye is not a consideration; with luck this will be your only wedding.

If the dye job simply won't give you a near enough match and the new fabric leaps out visually, consider covering the inserts with some sort of decoration. Victorian and Edwardian dresses are usually heavily decorated to begin with. Ivory-colored lace bands or ecru embroidery might be appliquéd on or glued in place over the inserts and then dotted with pearls. If you decide to add decoration, work with the entire dress in mind so your revisions look balanced.

Restyling an older wedding dress is another possible alternative, depending on your sewing skills. Necklines can be lowered or filled in, sleeves added or removed, and fullness subtracted from skirts. Sketch how you want the finished product to look and leave your drawing in some highly visible place for a few days just to make sure it's what you really want. If your sketch looks more complicated than the skills available to you,

check prices from local tradespeople who do alterations.

Pretty prom dresses from the '50s and '60s are popping up in antique clothing boutiques and can be transformed into great wedding dresses. Many are strapless, held up by featherboning sewn into the side seams. Strapless might be a bit bare for the ceremony but fine for the reception. Lace or satin bolero jackets, easily made from retail patterns, are a good choice for a cover and were part of the styling of those decades.

Many brides truly yearn for a wedding gown with a long train. This, too, can be added over any basic floor-length dress. Trains are attached to the dress at the shoulders, the waist, or the hips if the dress has a dropped waist. If a waist or hip train fits your fancy, you have your choice of making the train cover the entire skirt, curve back from a center front opening, or simply be attached at the sides and fall from the back waist seam only. Access to a dress form will make the construction of a train much easier. If no form is available, find a patient friend who will stand in the dress for fittings so the train will fall gracefully.

A detachable train is an option and makes moving around the reception easier. You'll have the fun of the big train during the ceremony yet won't be bothered lugging it around the rest of the day. Detachable shoulder trains are often sewn onto the gown by a few tiny stitches that may be snipped after all formal photographs are taken and the reception line disbands. Waist and skirt trains can be made as overskirts, on their own waistbands, and can be removed when the party begins.

COSTUMES

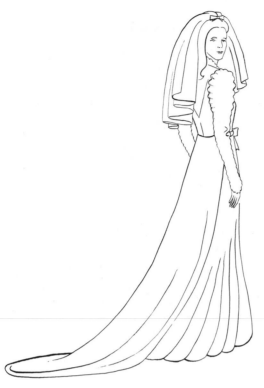

Detachable train

An alternate to a detachable train, if the styling of your gown permits, is to "bustle" the train. Small fabric loops hook up to small buttons near the back waist to form a bustle effect, creating a soft pouf of fabric across the lower back of the garment. The silhouette becomes deliciously Victorian, and the additional fabric of the train becomes manageable. Again, access to a dress form or a patient friend who will help with the fitting is most necessary.

▲▲▲▲▲▲▲

ACCESSORIES

▼▼▼▼▼▼▼

There are many choices open to you for the head coverings for the bride and her attendants. Hat frames or hat bases are available in most small cities or by mail from some of the sources listed below. The frames or bases often are made of white buckram, a stiffened fabric that must be covered with one of your wedding fabrics before it becomes wearable. Either hand stitch or glue the fabric onto the buckram, using a craft adhesive designed for fabrics. Test a strip of scrap material before you tackle the hat base to make sure the adhesive doesn't affect the color. Cover the frame completely and then add flowers, ribbons, veiling, or decorations as you go. Be lavish. "Delectable" is a good word to keep in mind when you're making wedding hats.

From Kathy Fredericks' notebook we get the following companies as mail-order sources for trimmings and notions:

Manny's Millinery Supply
63 West 38th Street
New York, NY 10018
Telephone: 212-840-2235 or 2236
Quarterly catalogs for hat bases, fabric flowers, feathers, veiling, and trims

A. Baer
515 East Market Street
Louisville, KY 40202
Telephone: 502-583-5521
Catalog has rhinestones, feathers, sequins, trims, rhinestone and bead motifs

Newark Dressmaker Supply
6473 Ruch Road
P. O. Box 2448
Lehigh Valley, PA 18001
Telephone: 215-837-7500
Threads, trims, ribbons, lace, eyelet, patterns, and other craft supplies

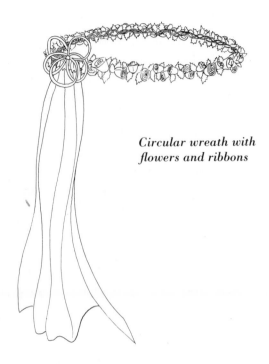

Circular wreath with flowers and ribbons

You may decide to have the attendants wear floral wreaths instead of hats. Artificial flowers and leaves are a good choice for the headgear, as long as they echo the live flowers everyone will be carrying. They can be done weeks in advance, perhaps at a party where each attendant does her own.

Wreaths can be constructed simply by sewing small flowers, leaves, and ribbons onto a wider satin ribbon, which each attendant ties around her head. For some hairstyles a plastic headband can serve as a base. Cover the plastic with the same fabric the dresses are made from and then decorate with sewn-on flowers, leaves, and ribbons.

For a more stable, full-circle wreath, use fabric-covered millinery wire, purchased from a notions and trimmings store. Several lengths of milliner's wire should be twisted together, forming a circlet that fits comfortably on the head. Weave narrow ribbons around the wire,

leaving long streamers at the back. The ribbons can be knotted, braided, and so forth. Finally, stitch small flowers and artificial leaves onto the circlet, making sure each wreath is about the same fullness. Tie the streamers together at the back, covering up any cut edges where the wire was joined.

Research fashion magazines for other headdress ideas. Almost anything can qualify as a headcovering, from bows to headache bands. Millinery supply shops generally carry large barrettes that are wonderful bases for head ornaments, as are the expandable combs from the dime store. Use wide strips of fabric stiffened with spray starch, or use stiffened ribbons and sew or wire pouffy bows and loops onto a comb or barrette:

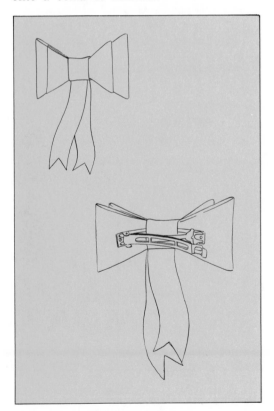

Barrette with double ribbon bows

COSTUMES

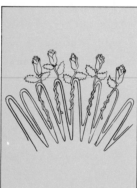

*Flexible comb with
artificial flowers
wired on*

Purchase veiling by the yard, cut to the size and shape you want, and machine sew lace edging around the edge for a pretty bride's veil. Attach the finished veil with a few tiny stitches to whatever hat or headcovering you choose, so it will remain securely in place for the ceremony. For a round or oval veil, fold the veiling double and then in half, as shown below.

Pretty rosebuds and small roses can be made out of strips of the dress fabric and used on headgear and accessories. See directions in Chapter 11, Decor and Props.

Gloves used to be considered a necessity for the bride and her attendants, back when everybody wore gloves all the time to look ladylike. They are no longer required but can be worn if you choose to. Just be sure they are color matched to the dresses for visual unity.

An alternative to gloves is fabric or lace mitts, covering forearms, wrists, and hands but leaving the fingers uncovered.

For an oval or round bride's veil:

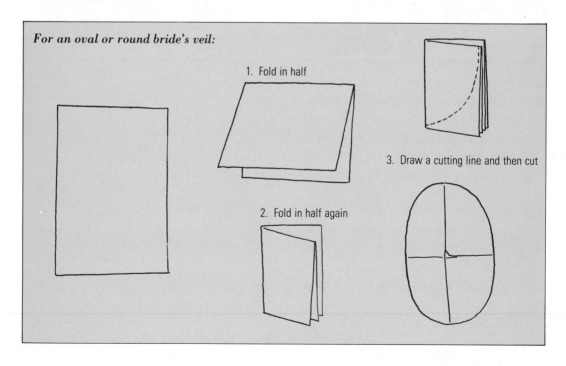

1. Fold in half
2. Fold in half again
3. Draw a cutting line and then cut

Mitts are most effective when worn with short-sleeved or sleeveless dresses and must be color coordinated to look as though they belong with the costumes.

Mitts are made easily from Kathy Fredericks' directions:

Trace each attendant's hand and forearm onto a piece of paper. Trace up to the first knuckle on fingers and thumb so there will be enough fabric to turn the raw edges under; also add extra length on the arm for turnover. Then add a ½-inch seam allowance on the sides and thumb hole. Beginning at the wrist, add an extra seam allowance going up the arm. The amount of extra seam allowance will vary from arm to arm, depending on how plump the arm is; an inch on each side is usually sufficient.

Cut out the pattern from a doubled piece of scrap fabric, pin it together, and try it on for fit. Mitts should not be form-fitting! When it feels comfortable, take the pattern, cut two out for each hand, reversing the pattern to get a left and a right. Handstitch the turned-under edges for a clean finish.

Finalize your plans as much as you can before you hold your bridesmaids' luncheon session. Bring as many visuals as you can round up so that everybody present can immediately grasp the overall production picture. Describe your visualization completely, adding sound and light descriptions. Show your fabric collage color board and any patterns you've purchased or sketches you've done. Be detailed in your presentation; include the jewelry (if included) on the attendants, shoes, hose if visible, and headgear. Work for "oohs" and "aahs" from your audience; let your enthusiasm carry the day!

Mitts

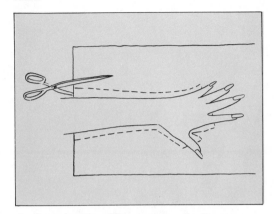

1. *Trace hand and forearm to make the pattern. Cut two pieces for one hand; turn the pattern over and cut two more for the other hand.*

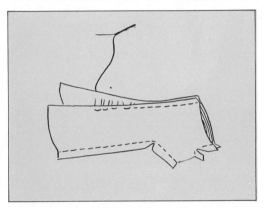

2. *Stitch two pieces together—right sides of the fabric together. Clip with scissors. Turn right side out. Hem the raw edges.*

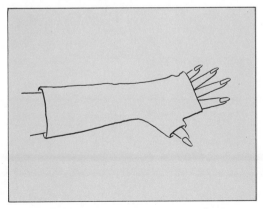

3. *Finished mitt.*

C O S T U M E S

▼ *The Costume worksheets can be found on pages 206–7.*

▲▲▲▲▲▲▲

8

FLOWERS

▼▼▼▼▼▼▼

▼▼▼▼▼▼▼

F L O W E R S

According to Ralph Stivali, talented New York City party designer, there are two important things to keep in mind when you are planning your wedding: "First, let it be what you want your wedding to be. There are going to be many people tugging at you, saying, 'It should be this, it should be that,' but there are no rules here. It should be what you want it to be, what really works for you. And second and most important, stay within your budget!"

To many of us, flowers and weddings are synonymous. We think of tables laden with massive floral arrangements and wedding bouquets lavish with blooms. Unfortunately, flowers quickly become a major expense if you buy them to use with a free hand. The trick is to use flowers and greenery judiciously, to create magic effects while still staying within the budget.

Your color scheme and the overall "look" of the wedding are the departure points for planning the flowers. Every element in your production must be designed to add to the viewer's understanding of your point of view—from the flowers the bridal party wears and carries to the flower arrangements that decorate the rooms and the tables. Refer to your workbook Concept, page 190, and the fabric boards you did (for the costume chapter) for guidance.

And remember, there is no one perfect flower. You are working to create a total visual effect by adding appropriate flowers to the costumes and the wedding space. Once you know your concept and your colors, use the Flowers workbook sheet on page 207 and begin to list all available seasonal flowers and greens that might fit in. Seasonal is the important word. These are the flowers that are abundant and therefore less expensive than out-of-season varieties.

Judith Cocke, the guiding hand behind Zen Florist, newsworthy Texas floral designers headquartered in Dallas, recommends doing some research before you attempt to organize your flowers. "Everybody loves beautiful flowers," she says, "but few people outside of the trade look at floral pieces to see how they are designed, what makes them work."

Spend a little library time looking through all the current home magazines and the bride's magazines to see what is current in floral design. Judy makes special mention of *Architectural Digest* and *Interior Design Magazine* for source material on the latest looks in flowers. Look at the spacing of large and small blossoms, how the colors are mixed, and how the shape of the grouping is achieved. When you come across bouquets and/or decorative arrangements you like, photocopy them to use as reference material. This

might seem like the last thing you want to spend your time on, but flowers are too important to leave to chance.

Once you have completed the research, arrange a meeting with the person who has volunteered to do your flowers. It's vital that the flower person be totally in accord with your plans. If you fear the volunteer might take off in his or her own direction, give the person a mini-version of your fabric boards (see the Costumes chapter) and the photocopies you got from the library. Since you have chosen the volunteer for already-proven skills, take care to offer the research material as a help rather than a prototype you want slavishly copied. Your volunteer's creativity is what will make or break the final product, so handle with care!

The flowers and greenery you choose can come from people's gardens, local florists, wholesale flower markets, or they can be wild flowers cut from nearby fields. Anything goes if it fits into your production plan.

. . .

Let's focus on the bridal party flowers first. The bouquet the bride carries sets the tone for the rest of the assemblage. The attendants carry scaled-down versions of the bride's flowers using fewer choice blooms or a more limited selection. The men's boutonnieres may be of one of the blossoms from the bride's bouquet; the altar flowers and aisle ribbon blossoms will match something in the bride's bouquet, and the flower girl will have the same flowers in her tiny basket. Both mothers can carry or wear coordinating flowers, if you choose to have them include flowers in their outfits.

F L O W E R S

FLOWERS

▲▲▲▲▲▲▲▲

HOW TO MAKE YOUR OWN GREAT-LOOKING BOUQUETS

▼▼▼▼▼▼▼

To make the bride's (and other) bouquets, simply tie the bouquet loosely together with pretty, coordinating ribbons or use a plastic bouquet holder form purchased from a local florist or supply shop.

THE TIED-RIBBON BOUQUET

Alan Boehmer, design partner in Madderlake, one of New York City's leading floral design firms, uses the tied-ribbon method and recommends it highly for cosmopolitan, elegant bouquets. Working with an assistant three or four hours before the wedding, Alan composes each bouquet himself.

"I always do it in front of a mirror," Alan says, "and I hold the bouquet myself as I'm assembling it. I have a vase of the assorted flowers I'm going to use nearby. I start with some bigger, filler pieces, perhaps some lilac, or some wax flower, something that's nice and fluffy. Then I start stuffing in flowers but always look in the mirror because that will be the front view of the bouquet. I fill it out and then I hold it and have someone tie it with a ribbon, leaving the stems on. I immediately cut them and put them in water.

"If there are to be ribbon streamers, I like to use a very narrow, good satin. I make up a lot of loose, loopy bows with a lot of long streamers, tie them together, and then tie that to the bouquet. Other flowers are tied into the streamers: sprigs such as lilies of the valley, stephanotis, or

little bits of flowers that are already in the bouquet. They are tied in with pretty little square knots. Sometimes I tie extra knots into the streamers known as love knots, and they're traditional. Actually, the extra knots weigh down the streamers so they hang better.

"If you are working with very narrow ribbons, you might braid them, which is pretty. Make the streamers nice and long for the bride and shorter for the bridesmaids. I believe in spending some money on the ribbon. It's so important. Match the color to the dresses—exact match or a complimentary color. Mix the ribbon fabrics; use some satin or taffeta, as long as it all goes together."

Alan makes up the bouquets three or four hours before the ceremony and keeps them in water as long as he can. "I like to dry off the stems and hand them to the wedding party as they start down the aisle," he says with a laugh.

Judy Cocke recommends using masses of any one beautiful flower if you have access to unlimited cutting gardens. "An armload of blue delphiniums tied with a wide white satin bow with long streamers is hard to beat," says Judy. "Or masses of medium-sized roses held together with pretty ribbon. You'll achieve a natural, fresh look similar to what the European floral designers are doing, and it's terrific!"

For a more formal ribbon bouquet, Judy designs her bride's bouquets around one central flower, such as a butterfly orchid or a perfect gardenia. The main flower is combined with two other prominent flowers, each of a different shape, giving variety to the design. If the central flower is an orchid, for example, it might be used with medium-sized open roses. Then Judy might choose freesia or Queen Anne's Lace to add a lacy, long-stemmed look. The finished bouquet is tied with a ribbon with long streamers to achieve a casual but sophisticated look.

"Also, it's important to make a large bunch of flowers as stable as possible so they won't start spilling out on the way to the altar. Wrap a few turns of florist's tape around the stems, binding them all together, and then cover the wrap with the ribbons. Florist's tape is inexpensive, comes in green and brown, is about ½ inch wide, and is slightly stretchy. Florists or floral supply and craft stores carry florist's tape.

"Never use regular white roses," she cautions. "They tend to look green and bruise very easily. There's a white rose from Holland called the Bridal White Rose that has a pink tint to it and looks wonderful. But whatever you use, work for fullness. You want the bouquets to look opulent, not skimpy."

Judy mentions the need to "condition" or "harden off" flowers and greens before using them. Conditioning is one of those trade secrets most of us don't know anything about, and it's vital if you are going to cut or arrange the flowers yourself. Basically, fresh-cut flowers often droop and look limp if they are put immediately into arrangements. Cut flowers look better and last longer if the stems, flowers, and leaves are allowed to become filled with water before use.

A rudimentary way to condition is to cut everything in the very early morning or late evening when the stems are naturally full of water. Cut the stems diagonally with a clean, sharp knife (no

scissors) and place them, without crowding, in deep pails of warm water. Try for baby-bottle temperature for the water; that is, close your eyes and drop some warm water on the inside of your wrist. If you can't tell exactly when the water hits, then it's the perfect temperature for feeding baby or for conditioning flowers. Place the pails in a cool, dark spot and leave overnight or for at least a few hours. Then arrange them, but try to keep the arrangements in a cool place until needed.

There's a lot more to conditioning than the above data, should you want to get into it. Some flowers react best to slightly acid or slightly alkaline water, and so forth. Fortunately, there's a wonderful and inexpensive book that explores the subject in most usable form: *Gardening for Flower Arrangement*, written by Arno and Irene Nehrling and published by Dover Publications, Inc.*

Judy Cocke also has good advice on caring for store-bought flowers if you don't have access to a cutting garden. "If you're going to buy the flowers yourself," she advises, "first find out when the store bought them. Try to get them the day before the wedding. If you can do that, then take wads of toilet paper, soak them in water, lay them on top of the flowers, and place the whole container in a cooler overnight. Usually 40 to 42 degrees is good, like the bottom of one's home refrigerator or a Styrofoam cooler with a chill pack buried in it under newspaper.

"The next day put the flowers in water

*If you can't locate the book, write to: Department Gardening, Dover Publications, Inc., 180 Varick Street, New York, NY 10014.

F L O W E R S

81

FLOWERS

for a few hours. If they haven't opened enough, cut the stems on a slant and place them in deep, warm water. It shoots up the stems and makes the flowers open quickly. Then do the ribbons just before the ceremony.

MORE FORMAL BOUQUETS

Using the bouquet holder forms is a no-fail way to make more formal bouquets. The form consists of a round cake of flor-ist's clay (*oasis* is a commercial name) en-cased in a plastic basket with a handle coming down off it. The oasis is damp-ened and the flowers inserted into it, creating whatever design you choose.

The forms are available from florists, floral supply shops, and many craft sup-ply stores. They cost about three or four dollars each and come in a variety of sizes. Decorative covers with gathered lace edgings are also available to slip the form into, providing a frilly frame for the bouquet.

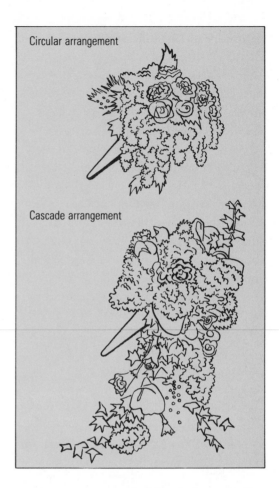

Circular arrangement

Cascade arrangement

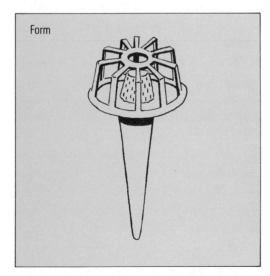

Form

Bouquet holder with oasis—insert flower stems into porous cake that has been dampened.

The forms can be used for circular bouquets or for cascades, depending on the choice and placement of the flowers and greenery. Small garden ivy works wonderfully for a cascade, interspersed with Alan Boehmer's knotted, blossom-bedecked ribbons. Design the bouquets in front of a mirror or by working directly in front of the form, starting with the bride's flowers. Once the bride's bouquet is put together and you love it, do lesser ver-sions for the attendants. Since the oasis is dampened, the flowers will look fresh for several hours at least.

The oasis is the basis for the flower girl's basket. Cut a small block of oasis and tape it into a plastic bag fitted into

Flower girl basket

the bottom of the tiny basket. The rest of the basket, except for the live flowers, can be decorated several days in advance, using ribbon streamers, knots, and bows to relate it to the other wedding flowers. Shortly before the ceremony, dampen the oasis, insert the flowers, and it's ready to go.

▲▲▲▲▲▲▲

ALTAR AND TABLE FLOWERS

▼▼▼▼▼▼▼

The altar flowers can be handled in any number of ways. If your ceremony is going to take place in a church or synagogue, the clergyman will fill you in on the rules for sanctuary flowers. If there are no hard-and-fast rules, you can create a large floral arrangement for the focal point using any attractive tall container; the same kind of arrangement you would have as a focal point in your home. By flanking the arrangement with tall tapers you can suggest an altar effect without going any further.

Garlands draped around the "altar" table are another possibility and can be made easily at home several days before the ceremony. Use a piece of string to drape around the table, setting the depths of each festoon, and then measure the string for the length of garland you'll need.

Garlands can be constructed from any greenery that is rather small-scale and relatively full. Dried straw, wheat and grain sheaves can also be used, giving a crisp, Nordic garland that works well with dried and artificial flowers for winter weddings.

Cut 3-inch to 6-inch snips of the greens and bunch some together in your hand. Using very fine florist's wire, wrap a few turns around your bunch and leave the wire hanging. Add another clump of greens, spacing it so it overlaps the first. Wrap that with wire so it extends over the first bunch. Keep adding bunches and reinforcing with wire until you have made the length you need.

Mist lightly and place in a large plastic bag punched with a few holes so some air can get in. Keep in a relatively cool place until it's time to decorate the altar. Tape or wire the garland in place, adding fresh flowers after it is secured. Choose sturdy flowers to insert in the garland if you can, since there will be no water source to keep them perky.

Florist's bows can add a festive air to the garland and can be made up in ad-

F L O W E R S

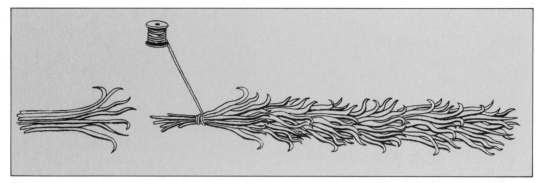

Greenery garland

Florist's bow

Step 1: *Make a loose knot in the middle of the ribbons.*

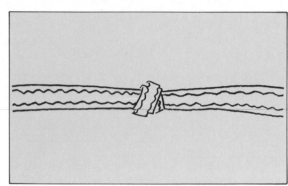

Step 2: *Twist wire around the center of a series of large loops you have gathered. Once the loops are secured together, fan them out.*

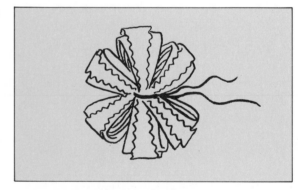

Step 3: *Place the loop unit over the knot made in Step 1 and attach it by twisting the wire (used to secure the loops) through the back of the knot.*

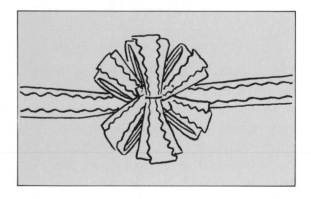

vance. The bows are even more effective when doubled, using a wide ribbon with a narrower ribbon placed on top of it. Try a wide satin with either a narrower lace ribbon or a taffeta ribbon with a picot edge. Depending on the size of the bows, you'll need about 3 yards of each ribbon per bow plus some of the florist's wire.

Cut a yard of each, center the narrow on the wide, and make a loose knot in the center of the strips. Set aside. Gather the remaining ribbons, centered, into large loops and twist a bit of wire around the middle of the loops, dividing them in half. Place the knot of the yard-long ribbon "strip" you set aside over the wire securing the three loops together and bend the loose ends of the securing wire through the back of the knot. To hold it fast twist in the back to secure the bow, and fan the loops out to make them full and puffy. Attach to the garland with extra wire twisted into the greenery. Hang extra streamers, knotted and with flowers, from the bows if desired.

Table decorations play an important role in setting the stage for the wedding party. Ralph Stivali says, "When decorating a party room you need to work for in-

stant reactions. You have only about thirty seconds to capture your audience when they walk into the party space. Visual impact is what it's all about."

He suggests letting your budget be your guide in the initial table design. Choose one or two stalks of very dramatic flowers or larger amounts of field flowers such as daisies and baby's breath. Or work all in white for a rich effect on a tight budget. The use of fabrics and thin ribbons in your table decorations is very important and can extend the flower colors out over the tabletops, adding impact to a small amount of blooms.

One of Ralph's trademarks is his use of fabrics to cover ordinary nonmatching candleholders and small vases. Choose an interesting fabric, perhaps a metallic version of one of your wedding colors. Using pinking shears, cut small squares of cloth and fold them over the base of the candleholder or vase. Tie the fabric in place with several color-coordinated thin ribbons and swirl the ribbon streamers around the table. Group a combination of candles and single flowers in bud vases on each table, with the holders covered with fabric and lots of ribbons.

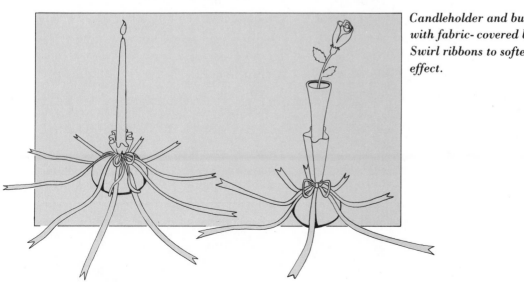

Candleholder and bud vase with fabric-covered bases. Swirl ribbons to soften the effect.

FLOWERS

A Stivali variation on this is to use several very long tapers in fabric-covered bases with graceful lengths of ivy twined around the candles. Finish with ribbons to create a footing on the table:

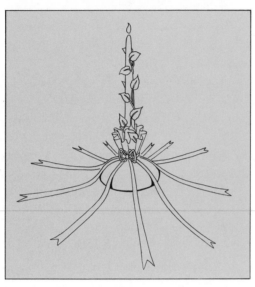

Candle with ivy in fabric-covered holder. Swirl ribbons to soften the effect.

Spray painted greenery may be used in combination with natural colored greens to create exciting table decorations that can bypass totally the need for cut flowers. "It's not that difficult," says Ralph. "It's just a matter of getting your hands dirty. Work with leaves or greens that are absolutely dry and use a good-quality spray paint. Krylon is a good brand. Metallic sprays are very successful. Spray a few leaves gold, and use the rest green. Or use silver, gold, or black for a wonderful effect that won't look low-budget."

Use your initial library research to help with your table design. Also refer to the chapters on food and decor for presentation information. In order to pull the re-

ception room together, make the guests' table flowers mini versions of the large displays for the buffet and food tables.

If your overall wedding theme is trendy and sophisticated, you can go modern/minimalist, highlighting relatively few flowers by placing them in dramatic settings. Judy Cocke suggests renting several huge glass bubble vases for the serving tables and then buying the necessary number of small, inexpensive glass bubble vases for the guests' tables. Choose large, rather exotic flowers or sprays such as bird of paradise and place several of them in each huge bubble. Repeat with smaller versions for the guests' tables, scattering a handful of beach pebbles or fishtank gravel in the bottom of each bubble. Then buy mirror tiles from a home improvement center, place the mirrors under the bubbles, and swirl some silver glitter dust on the mirrors and surrounding tablecloths for a finishing touch.

Country garden weddings can use table versions of the flower girl's basket, with flowers and greens inserted into wet florist's oasis. For best effect put enough greenery in each basket so the oasis is completely covered and let the greenery flow over the sides and onto the cloth. Candles, either tall tapers or small votive candles in low glass cups, are wonderful for tables and can be tucked into wreaths formed from grapevines or sturdy lengths of ivy.

For truly low-budget table flowers with lots of charm, Judy Cocke recommends laying in a supply of inexpensive dried sheet moss, available from your florist, and cans of spray glue. Collect a group of identical containers, such as old milk cartons or big juice cans. Using a newspaper pattern, cut out pieces of the moss and spray glue them onto the containers, completely covering the outsides. Put blocks of oasis in the covered containers and insert greenery, ribbons and bows, balloons, flowers, or what-have-you, to create pretty centerpieces for the guests' tables. Cover larger boxes or tubes with moss for the buffet tables. Be sure to glue ivy leaves around the top of each container so no edges show.

The moss cover will work wonders on terra-cotta flowerpots, wooden containers, anything that will accept spray glue. If the container is not watertight, line it with a plastic bag or set a jar filled with water inside, making sure it is not visible to the guests. Styrofoam blocks and shapes sold in craft shops and sewing departments can be covered with moss. Styrofoam shapes have an extra advantage: Candles can be pushed down securely into them. Use bobèches, the glass drip catchers, for safety since Styrofoam releases toxic fumes if burned.

Madderlake is known for its innovative table pieces, often used as props in major fashion and home magazines. Alan Boehmer says they are concerned with the visibility at each guest table; no table arrangement should interfere with all guests' being able to talk across the table. His rule of thumb places a 10-inch height limit on table pieces for adult parties. Low baskets holding a combination of fruits and flowers and weighted down with pebbles are a favorite combination, relating to the food table decorations. Cover the base first, he suggests, and then add your flowers for effect.

An alternative to the 10-inch-high arrangements are tall, thin cylinder or to-piary tree table pieces, where the bulk of the arrangement sits on top of a pole, above the heads of the guests. Guests can still talk freely across the table and enjoy innovative floral designs besides. To make topiary trees collect big plastic bucket containers, one per table. Mix up plaster of paris, fill the containers equally, and set lengths of pole into the center of each, to harden upright, forming the tree trunks. Let dry until hard, then remove and discard the plastic.

Place large Styrofoam balls or round shapes made from chicken wire and covered with gauze securely on each pole to form the tree. Cover with strips of sheet moss, spray glued into place. Insert dried or artificial flowers into the trees, plus ribbons and streamers, color coordinated to the rest of the event.

Topiary tree table piece

FLOWERS

F L O W E R S

Topiary table arrangement with flowers, ribbons, and tulle

Alan described one other tall arrangement he had done that was a particular favorite. He made bases, like the topiary tree bases, and wired small platforms on the tops of the poles. Each platform held a wired-on container with a pretty flower arrangement set in it. To camouflage the bases he took yards of white tulle, draped it down to cover the pole and plaster base, and gathered it back up into an airy pouf held in place with ribbons and streamers.

"It was almost like a Maypole," Alan said, "with these huge arrangements on top, spilling down. Bridal wreath was available at that point, and I tied it all up with pink and white ribbons. It was just

beautiful, and the guests had no trouble seeing one another even though they were at tables for ten."

Madderlake has come out with a book entitled *Rediscover Flowers*, published by Stewart, Tabori and Chang, which promises to become one of the major reference books for floral design.

. . .

Both Alan and Judy offered the same summary suggestions to you and your flower volunteers: Agree on a plan, discuss all the details so there will be no rude surprises, and then stick to that plan no matter what else comes up!

▼ *The Flowers worksheets can be found on pages 208–9.*

▲▲▲▲▲▲▲

SOUND

▼▼▼▼▼▼▼

9

SOUND

The sound for your wedding has to fill two needs: to supply music and to function as a public address system. By manipulating the music, either live or tapes or records, you can somewhat control the actions of the guests. The ▼▼▼▼▼▼▼ public address part of the sound system will do the rest, calling the guests' attention to events such as the first dance and the cutting of the cake. Like all the other components of your wedding, choosing the right sound is important enough to merit your attention.

The music for your celebration will probably encompass classical, semi-classical, or cocktail lounge sound and popular dance music. Few of us have a working vocabulary of all genres of music, so seek advice from others when you plan the programs. If no friend or relative is knowledge-able enough to guide you, consider a brief paid consultation with a music professional who is expert in the areas you don't know about.

▲▲▲▲▲▲▲

THE MUSIC

▼▼▼▼▼▼▼

The choice between live music and electronic music depends on your budget. Live music is more expensive but brings a lot of excitement to any event. On the other hand, taped music brings you your choice of the greatest artists and finest recordings the world has to offer and costs less. The best of all possibilities, of course, is to have marvelously talented friends who volunteer to play for you. If that's not possible, you must look elsewhere.

A word of caution: With the choice of music, as with the choices of all the other elements of your celebration, make sure it's what you really want. Don't be coerced into letting a family member supply the music unless it happens to be the music of your choice. I've attended two weddings that were made less than wonderful because the music was supplied by Dad's amateur jazz band and Brother's college buddies' pickup group. Don't field an ego trip for relatives. It's your day, so make it really work for you!

Most churches and temples have their own sound systems, personnel, and rules for usage. When you have your pre-wedding meeting with the clergy, you will clarify all that. Be sure you understand the fees involved for the organist and any soloists or choir who might participate. You will be given some choice of selections to be played or hymns to be sung. In most cases the music will be taken care of for you if you don't want to design it yourselves.

A logical compromise for the non-church wedding is to combine live and electronic sound, hiring your favorite group to play for dancing and using tapes and records for the formal parts of the celebration. Very few dance bands can handle the ceremonial music with any flair. It's really better to use a clear, crisp recording of, say, Purcell's "Trumpet Voluntary" for the aisle walk than to listen to the local group groping its way through the "Wedding March" from *Lohengrin*.

If your ceremony will take place at home or in rental space, you can design your own sound, combining live and electronic as you see fit. A small string or wind ensemble, a pianist, or a harpist can add great charm to the ceremony, followed by taped Cole Porter for cocktails and recorded dance music for the party.

A good source for inexpensive live music is any local music school or college music department. Student musicians are often of professional caliber and are delighted to get the work. Be sure you hear their music before any deal is made, and check any references you are given. You need them to be prompt and efficient as well as young and talented.

Once you've located your music source and agreed on a program, fee, and length of performance, draw up a simple letter of agreement outlining the deal. This can be typed or handwritten, with a carbon so each of you has a copy. The wording should be something like this:

[Date]

Dear _____,

This letter is to confirm our arrangement for you [and your group] to play at our wedding on Saturday, June 20,

S O U N D

SOUND

198-. You and [name the other performers] will arrive between 1 and 1:30 P.M. at the Grange Hall [address], and be ready to play at 2 P.M.

We agreed on the Chopin and Liszt for openers, and the Mendelssohn and Wagner for the marches. The rest of the music is up to you and will be similar in style.

You will play until 3:30 P.M. when the food service will begin, taking a 10-minute break every half hour. We hope you will join us for the buffet and the rest of our party.

The fee will be $20 per musician. Enclosed is a deposit of $30; the balance is to be paid after the wedding. Please sign and return one copy of this letter for our files.

Sincerely,

(Them) _____   (You) _____

If you decide to skip live music, see if you can recruit a volunteer or two to run the sound at your wedding. Work with them to orchestrate the entire celebration, using classical and light classics for the ceremony and cocktail part of the reception and incorporating your favorites when the dancing begins. Many public libraries have records and tapes that can be borrowed, giving you access to large collections of the world's greatest music.

▲▲▲▲▲▲▲

THE SOUND SYSTEM

▼▼▼▼▼▼▼

Rental halls often have their own sound system or at least a speaker's microphone hookup that will simplify your planning.

You will need a P.A. system no matter what, so use any equipment that is offered. Adding music can be done separately by the stereo buffs among your family and friends. (Refer to the chapter on lighting for data on assessing the power available to you in your building.)

West Coast audio engineer Norman Brazell, head sound person for the Bay Area's Berkeley Square night club, says to start by figuring out how big a sound system you need to construct for your celebration. Norman's rule of thumb for both indoor and outdoor parties is one watt per person for good sound coverage.

Let's backtrack a minute. Home stereo systems consist of four parts: a sound source, that is, a turntable and/or tape-deck; an amplifier; two speakers, maybe more.

Amplifiers are the key to the numbers you'll need. (For the novices among us, amplifiers are the component parts that have all the tuning knobs in front and often include AM-FM radios. The amplifier receives the sound from either a record player or a tape deck and passes on the sound to the speakers.)

You'll see on the back of your amplifier how many watts the amplifier has. An inexpensive home set has between fifteen and thirty watts; a more expensive set has between thirty and sixty watts; and so on. Thus, if your amplifier has fifty watts written on the back of it, you have good sound for a party of fifty people. Any number over that necessitates additions to your system.

Refer to your guest list and count up how many watts you're going to need, then check other people's stereos. Borrow enough amplifiers, with their speakers, to

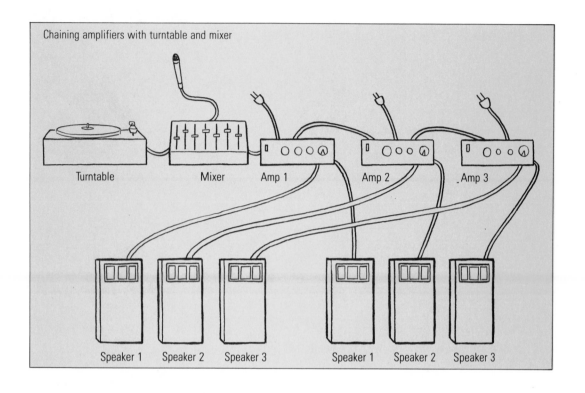

Chaining amplifiers with turntable and mixer

Turntable   Mixer   Amp 1   Amp 2   Amp 3

Speaker 1   Speaker 2   Speaker 3   Speaker 1   Speaker 2   Speaker 3

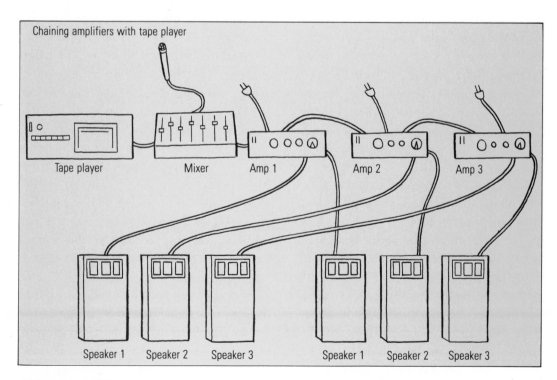

Chaining amplifiers with tape player

Tape player   Mixer   Amp 1   Amp 2   Amp 3

Speaker 1   Speaker 2   Speaker 3   Speaker 1   Speaker 2   Speaker 3

Chaining amplifiers

S O U N D

SOUND

Four-speaker placement

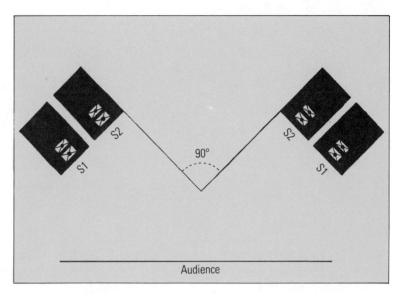

cover the number of guests you're expecting. You'll probably end up with three or four sets connected to one another. "Chained together" is the pro terminology —you will rig up a chain of amps, as many as you need, for good sound.

Look again at the back of your amplifier. You'll see a series of small openings labeled "Tape In" and "Tape Out" or "Record In" and "Record Out." Newer, state-of-the-art sets might have "Pre-Amp In" and "Pre-Amp Out" on the back. These openings are where you connect up the other stereo sets.

Go to a stereo equipment store and buy one phono jack for each set you're adding. The phono jacks, also called RCA phono jacks, are generally used with tape decks —not to be confused with phone jacks for telephone use! Phono jacks are electric wires with metal tips on both ends. To chain your stereo equipment together, plug one end of the phono jack into the "Tape Out" opening on your own amplifier and the other end of the phono jack into

the "Tape In" opening on another stereo amplifier.

Each of the amplifiers must be plugged into its own electric outlet and the volume tuned independently. Do not stack amplifiers on top of one another; they need air space around them to avoid overheating.

Norman recommends a two-point placement for the assorted speakers you'll have. This means grouping one set of speakers on one side of the room and the other set on the opposite side, angled to throw the sound into all parts of the party area. The crucial measurement on speaker placement is to aim for a 90-degree angle between speaker sets.

Speakers can be stacked up, creating small speaker towers such as those used in major outdoor concert amphitheaters. Speakers should always be placed 3 or 4 feet above the floor, around ear level. People are sound absorption units, according to Norman, and lower placement will sharply decrease the volume of your sound. If you are stacking speakers, begin by placing them on an elevated platform such as a card table or a wooden crate.

Speakers or a speaker tower can be covered with any thin, loosely woven fabric to coordinate with your decor. The fabric may be decorated with paint, stencils, appliqués, and so forth, to look festive, just as long as the cloth remains porous enough for good sound transmission.

Be sure to keep the speaker cables perpendicular to the amplifier cord that is plugged into an outlet. Even though all the cables are heavily insulated they still pick up from one another if they are placed parallel. Pull the speaker cables around to the front of the amplifiers, tape them together with masking tape to keep things tidy, and then run them out to the speakers, placed well in front of the amplifiers.

Leaving a sizable space between amps and speakers is vital if you plan to hook a speaker's microphone into the system. "Feedback" or "howl" is the dreadful noise produced by sound systems when the person using the microphone stands within the field of sound propagation, that is, in front of the speakers. Microphones can be rented inexpensively from equipment stores and will come with hookup instructions.

Another piece of equipment that might be fun to rent is a DJ mixer setup. This consists of two turntables plus a mixer that enables the sound person to fade music in and out from two records playing simultaneously. The DJ setup almost always includes a microphone since the "voice-over" is an important part of disco. The DJ mixer will come with instructions on hooking it up to your home stereo.

▲▲▲▲▲▲▲

THE MUSIC PROGRAM

▼▼▼▼▼▼▼

Gerb, the renowned DJ who has presided over the music at New York's Danceteria, suggests contacting local clubs or the sound person at your local radio station to find DJ rental equipment or to price hiring an experienced DJ to work the party. In larger cities the Yellow Pages often list DJs. Underground newspapers and college publications are also good to check.

Most DJs own their own equipment, including records, and will want to work out the program with you in advance. Gerb says each DJ has perfected his or her own style, so make every effort to hear the DJ in performance before you make any arrangements. Also, request references and check them.

Hiring a DJ for a five-hour job, including setup and breakdown time, can cost from fifty dollars up to thousands, so shop around and get comparative prices. Gerb warns us that tipping a DJ is considered an insult among the professionals; those who want to show appreciation can do so by taking up a collection at the very end of the party.

If you do select a DJ, meet several weeks before the party and give him or her a written outline for the program. If all the music is to be handled by the DJ, list the music and the performers you will want for the wedding marches, the incidental music to be played while the guests are being seated, and the cocktail music for the reception. Gerb says he likes to

S O U N D

SOUND

know the ages and dance preferences of the guests well in advance so he can locate and prepare a pleasing program.

Gerb cautions that finding a volunteer or two to run your sound is asking a great deal. The sound person cannot leave the equipment for any length of time and must be alert and working the entire reception. If two people agree to share the job, they should work out the division of time and activities well in advance so each will have time to enjoy the celebration.

A simpler alternative is to make your own tapes. Gerb recommends first-quality sixty-minute tapes such as TDK, Maxell, or Sony. These play thirty minutes per side and are stronger and more reliable than the one-hundred-twenty-minute tapes (sixty minutes per side). Begin planning your program with your guest list in hand. Music should be planned that is appropriate for every age group that will be at the party. Borrow as many records as you can and allow a few weeks to tape them. Mix fast and slow music and music from different eras on the same tapes so

that guests will not have to wait too long before their dance music comes up.

To make announcements over the microphone, fade the music out slowly and speak slowly and directly into the mike. Gerb firmly recommends practicing the fades and the announcing to develop a sense of pacing and a good, clear announcing voice. (Refer to Chapter 4, Protocol, for data on announcing the reception events.)

Gerb and Norman both suggest that the week before the wedding you assemble the entire sound system in somebody's garage and get it working at optimum. Once you're satisfied with the chainups and the type of sound, practice fading up and down and making announcements. Then tie large tags onto each piece of equipment, labeling it as to position and use. Make the labels as complete as necessary to ensure the on-location setup is quick, carefree, and accurate. Then pack up everything, including your carefully labeled tapes or records, and number the boxes. Your sound system is ready to go!

▼ *The Sound worksheet can be found on pages 210–11.*

▲▲▲▲▲▲▲

LIGHTING

▼▼▼▼▼▼▼

10

O*ddly enough, lighting is one of the most critical parts of your wedding, affecting the overall picture far more than the food, drinks, costumes, and props. Lighting can be a great manipulator, speeding us up or slowing us down, making us edgy, or soothing our souls.*

▼ ▼ ▼ ▼ ▼ ▼ ▼

Think about the illumination of a fast-food restaurant. The bright, glaring lights tell us to hurry up, this is not an eatery in which to linger. We emerge fed and ready to rush on to the next activity. By contrast, an elegant, candlelit dining room invites us to chat over our demitasse and perhaps order a liqueur to boot. We leave the dining room feeling fed, relaxed, and restored.

Lighting is also one of the most exciting elements you have to play with. Used creatively, lighting will transform an ordinary space into an enchanting place. But that's also the difficulty: How many of us understand lighting enough to think creatively about it? We need to develop an approach before we can go very far into design.

Paul Mathiesen, lighting designer and stage manager whose credits include New York's Palladium and Studio 54, says there are really two con-

siderations when lighting a wedding: The room must look pretty, and the people must look wonderful. "People want magic. The room must become a fairyland, with the guests all bathed in a warm glow. Elegant is the word everybody uses for weddings. Lighting is one of the few elements that can make it all happen."

Tom and Laura Herman, partners in Street Lighting, a well-known and highly creative New York City lighting design firm, tell us: "When we go into a space we look around and see how it can be changed from what it normally looks like. That's our point of view."

Tom continues, "We work to change the whole environment of the room. Certain things are important. For example, we look at any and all architectural details the space might have, because we know from experience these can be used as focal points. If a space has columns, arches, a fireplace, alcoves, we can highlight these and thus visually change the proportions of the space."

"Changing the look of the space is especially important if we're lighting a country club or someplace with which the guests are totally familiar. They've been in the dining room a million times, and it offers no surprises," Laura adds. "Then we come in. By creating a different look for the room we bring an excitement to the party. We create a bit of magic."

▲▲▲▲▲▲▲▲

THE APPROACH

▼▼▼▼▼▼▼

Let's begin our approach by considering some of light's better known qualities.

Light can be bright or dim, tightly focused or spilled out generously, colored or left clear. And it's highly movable; you can place light sources, from candles to lamps, almost anyplace you want, adding and subtracting illumination at will. By combining these qualities you can create your own magic. Contrast is what is important here. An evenly lighted space is rather boring. Think airports for the ultimate in boring lighting.

You have many techniques to work with. You can light from above, from below, or bounce light off reflective surfaces. You can spotlight areas or wash areas with light. Hundreds of colors are available to tint your light. You can project images, cast shadows, and outline spaces. And you have your choice of making, renting, or buying the equipment you'll need.

Greg Criscuolo, wearing his National Association of Broadcast Employees and Technicians union electrician's hat, suggests the best starting place for lighting design is at the fuse box that controls the power in your party space. "Before you spend any time thinking up fantasy effects, find out what you've got to work with. Once you've got the important figures in front of you, you can begin to get creative."

Greg tells us, "A professional electrician will check out the service with a clamp-on amp meter, which is an expensive piece of equipment. For purposes of the wedding, you can research your system and come up with a ball park figure with a built-in safety factor. It will take you a little longer, but an amp meter is too major a purchase to consider. Also, knowing what you've got electrically

LIGHTING

speaking is a good idea, whether or not you're staging a wedding."

Probably you will be able to get the electricity information for rented party space from the rental agent or building manager. You need to know how much power is available, divided into how many circuits, and which fixtures and plugs belong on which circuits. If no such information exists, use the following instructions from Greg for checking out your home power system.

Your home fuse box will have either small round fuses or a series of switches called circuit breakers. The rented party space is likely to have circuit breakers. Look on the switches or fuses and read the numbers printed there. These tell the amount of amperage that goes through your electrical service. In your home you might have a list like this:

20 amps
20 amps
15 amps
15 amps

Add up the numbers to get an amperage total. The above example will have 70 amps in the total service. This figure must be converted into wattage amounts before you can do much with it; the wattage ratings on the bulbs you use for your lighting are the important figures.

Greg gives us the following formula:

"For every 10 amps of power, you can have 1,000 watts of lighting equipment. This equation gives you a safety factor of about 8 percent, more than enough to withstand any voltage fluctuation that might damage your equipment."

The electrical service in any building is divided into circuits, each carrying a portion of the total service into some part of the building. The numbers on the fuses or on the circuit breakers tell you what you can count on for each circuit. Our example works out as follows:

20 amps	=	2,000 watts
20 amps	=	2,000 watts
15 amps	=	1,500 watts
15 amps	=	1,500 watts
70 amps	=	7,000 watts *Total Service*

Now that you know your totals you can begin to isolate each circuit, checking to see what is already drawing current. Your goal will be to find out which circuit(s) you can safely use for extra lighting and sound equipment for the wedding. Begin by turning on all the lights, radios, and so forth, in the rooms.

Checking circuits is best done by two people—one staying at the fuse or circuit breaker box and the other walking around the space to see what goes off when the circuit is broken. To break a circuit, simply flick the circuit breaker to the off position or unscrew a fuse.

Work with a pad and pencil, listing everything that goes off, room by room. Make a note of the wattage of each bulb that goes out. Once you've traced a circuit, add up the wattages in your notes. The total figure will tell you how much of the available service is being used. Subtract that from the wattage figure for that circuit, which you got from your fuse box exploration. The amount of wattage that is left over is what you have to work with for your light and sound equipment.

As an example: If you have a circuit

that delivers 1,500 watts and you find you are using light bulbs and appliances on that circuit totaling 745 watts, you have a little over 700 watts left on that circuit that you can use for special effects, that is, your sound system and lighting.

For large kitchen appliances, check the back of each unit to see the power used. The kitchen will be an important part of the party, however, so it's unwise to plan on using any power from the kitchen circuits. Any unused wattage might well go into extra coffee urns, hot trays, and so forth.

Once you know what power is available you can begin to plan your wedding party lighting. You will be perfectly safe as long as you keep track of how much you've used, how much you have left, and what power limits each piece of equipment you use can handle. Zip Cord, the common wires used on house lamps, is rated as to how much current it can handle safely. The higher the number of the Zip Cord, the less wattage it is designed to handle. When planning multiple lamp hookups it is *very important* to tell your hardware or electrical store salesperson what you want to do and ask for the appropriate merchandise.

Laura and Tom Herman use the power survey as the takeoff point for their lighting designs. "Get access to the space as early as you can," Laura suggests, "and work at the breaker box to see what figures each switch controls. We're usually in rental space, so we get a floor plan from the building agent and make our notes on that. Also, the rental agent will answer basic questions about rules for the space, such as whether we can change all the light bulbs if we want to."

You have already made your floor plan (see the chapter on locations) using the graph paper in the workbook. By now you know the type and placement of your tables, bars, and so forth, and have marked the electrical outlets, the existing lighting fixtures, and any architectural features in the space. And you have photocopied the plan several times so you have extra copies to work on.

Review your original wedding concept. The overall feeling must be carried out in the lighting plan; work for the total effect. A sunny garden feeling will require more lighting than a candlelit drawing room. Zero in on what you want the space to feel like and how everybody should look.

Paul, Greg, Tom and Laura each offered a similar, relatively easy, successful lighting design for indoor and outdoor weddings. Here are the three major parts, after which we'll explore each part in detail:

1) Begin with general, overall, low, even lighting for visibility. This assures you that people aren't going to stumble and that food and drink can be served graciously and efficiently. However, you don't need enough light to read by!

2) Integrate your special effects, highlighting or spotlighting focal points to give form to the room and direct the guests' attention to important features. This is where the creative part begins.

3) Finally, control the total illumination level in different parts of the space by the use of candles, massed in groups. Candlelight always says "party," adds romance, and makes people look wonderful.

LIGHTING

LIGHTING

▲▲▲▲▲▲▲▲

GENERAL LIGHTING

▽▽▽▽▽▽▽

The overhead lighting fixtures already in an indoor space are the first sources for general illumination. Chances are you won't be crazy about the existing fixtures unless your space has been specifically set up for parties. Meeting rooms, grange halls, and the like often have dreary fluorescents or glass-enclosed schoolroom fixtures. Some rooms have light coves that run around the edges of the walls at ceiling height, enclosing strips of fluorescent or incandescent lights that illuminate the ceiling.

The amount and kind of light the fixtures give off can be modified in a number of ways:

- Lower the wattage by unscrewing some of the bulbs.
- Replace existing bulbs with low-wattage and/or tinted bulbs.
- Use theatrical gels wrapped around fluorescents or placed over cove lighting to reduce the brightness and change color.
- Cover up incandescent fixtures with fabric shadelike constructions to soften and tint the light.

Let's talk now about theatrical lighting gels. These are transparent sheets of colored plastic, about 2 feet square, that are used to give color to stage lights. The name "gel" comes from gelatin; gels were made originally from actual gelatin, tinted to color while still liquid. When accidentally dampened, the old gels would liquefy in a most alarming manner!

Today's gels are sturdy plastic, come in about three hundred shades, and are relatively inexpensive. They can be cut with a scissors or mat knife and attached to the front of a lighting fixture by gaffer's tape, wire, or paper clips. Since the plastic sheet holds heat in, it is absolutely necessary to make pinholes in the face of the gel so that heat can escape. The holes are frequently made with a rotary pizza cutter, run in an X across the gel before it's put in place; however, ten or twelve widely spaced pinholes will do the job.

Laura and Tom Herman suggest approaching gel use with caution. "Be wary of gels," Laura says, "and go for the light color tints rather than the deep shades. Deep colors are tricky even for professional lighting designers. They cut down on the amount of light and can look garish rather than wonderful.

"Pale pinks and pale lavenders work best, and then only in combination with lots of white light. Avoid making all the general lighting any one color; it's the mix that makes the magic in a large space. In small spaces or for alcoves, and so forth, use only one tinted gel along with white light. For larger, focal-point spaces you

Gels are available from theatrical lighting stores or by mail order.

Rosco Labs, Inc. is a theatrical lighting manufacturer who supplies stores in every part of the country. They maintain a toll-free number to help customers locate the nearest distributor. If you have trouble finding a stage lighting supplier, call Rosco and get local referrals: 1-800-431-2338.

Mail-order catalogs are available from the following:

Stage Lighting Distributors Corp.
346 West 44th Street
New York, NY 10036

Times Square Theatrical &
Studio Supply Corp.
318 West 47th Street
New York, NY 10036

can use two tints, say pink and lavender, plus white."

Paul Mathiesen also mentions pale pink and pale lavender gels as his wedding color choices. "They both add a prettiness to a room that is unattainable with pure white light. Be careful, though, with pink gels on floral arrangements. The pink tint causes the green leaves to look kind of brown and unattractive. Lavender is a better choice for greenery."

To put gels on fluorescent fixtures, unfasten the grid or fixture cover, cut gels to fit into the available space, lay them in place, and put the cover back on. If there is no fixture cover, cut strips of gels and tape them onto the neon tubes, making sure the tape is not visible from below. Don't forget the pinholes for ventilation! To lower the illumination of fluorescents try removing one tube from each fixture and then gelling the remainder.

Barnett Simons, president of New York's Instant Interiors design consultation service, talks about unattractive lighting fixtures. "If the existing light fixtures are really the pits, you can cover them with inexpensive white umbrellas or parasols. Simply cut off the umbrella handle, fasten pretty ribbons in your colors at the tips, and tie the parasol directly below the ugly fixture. Then decorate with more streamers, flowers, and so on."

Another way to disguise unacceptable fixtures is to cover them with very thin muslin, either white, natural, or dyed to a pale tint of one of your wedding colors. New York's Gotham restaurant is a standout with elegantly draped fabric covers over old ceiling fixtures. The cover can be circular or angular in shape, depending on how you construct the framework. For

Parasol cover for light fixture

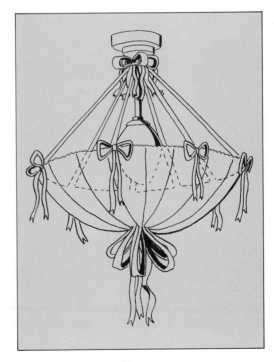

Fabric cover for light fixture

LIGHTING

LIGHTING

circular covers, buy hula hoops; cut wide strips of fabric, staple one end of each strip around the hoop, and gather the fabric so it drapes down evenly about a foot or so. Pull the cut ends to the center, tie with a string, and decorate with ribbons, and so forth.

General, low lighting for outdoor weddings calls for lighting equipment to be brought to the site, hung, and connected to extension cords from the nearest power source. Strings of Japenese lanterns are a charming answer to the lighting question and are easily fabricated at home.

Greg Criscuolo offers a basic explanations of terms for the novice electrician. There are many kinds of electrical plugs. You'll need to know those shown below.

Greg suggests you begin the lantern project by measuring the space to be lighted and figuring the distances to the nearest power source. Work on one of the photocopies of your outdoor floor plan, indicating what the lantern strings can be fastened to (trees, poles, and so on). Remember to keep track of the total power used by the strings of lights.

Space the lanterns 6 feet to 8 feet apart and draw the lantern placements in on your floor plan so you'll know how many to buy. Measure the length of the exten-

sion cords and try to borrow heavy-duty cords from camper or gardener friends. Do not use ordinary household extension cords!

Each string of lanterns is autonomous with its own sockets, bulbs, wire, and male plug that connects it to the power line. Your local hardware store will have the materials you need to make up the lantern strings. Bring along your floor plan, and be sure to discuss the entire project with a knowledgeable salesperson so you can be guided into buying the correct Zip Cord, line taps, and so forth. You'll need:

Enough Zip Cord to crisscross the space according to your drawing
One line tap (also called Click-Ons) for each lantern of a size that will fit on the Zip Cord
One male plug-in socket per lantern
One 40-watt bulb per lantern
Electrician's tape
One heavy-duty male plug for each string of lights
One heavy-duty female plug per string of lights

Lay out lengths of the proper gauge Zip Cord and cut to fit your floor plan. Wire a heavy-duty male plug onto one end of

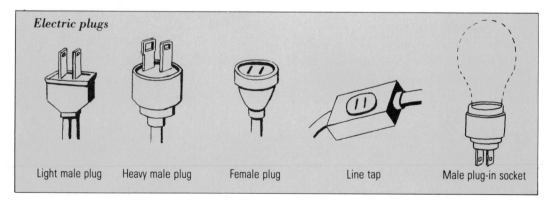

Electric plugs

Light male plug   Heavy male plug   Female plug   Line tap   Male plug-in socket

each length and a heavy-duty female plug onto the other end. Measure the lengths and mark where each lantern will be placed.

Following the directions on the female line taps, attach one at each place you want a lantern. Screw the 40-watt bulbs into the male plug-in sockets and plug them into the female line taps. You now have the basic lantern string:

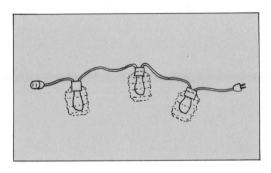

Japanese lantern string

Attach the paper lanterns, suspend the strings from the suspension points marked on your floor plan, and plug the end plug into a heavy-duty extension cord, using the electrician's knot:

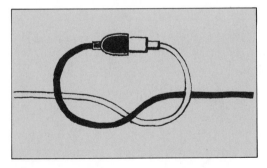

Electrician's knot

If you want some variation in light, you can paint some of the bulbs or some parts of the bulbs with ordinary nail polish, thinned down with polish remover if it's too thick to spread evenly.

▲▲▲▲▲▲▲

SPECIAL EFFECTS

▼▼▼▼▼▼▼

Once you have established the low-level, general lighting, you are ready to get into the special effects, adding dazzle to the space. Work off your floor plan, choosing spaces or things you want to highlight. The obvious focal points are the bride and groom's table, the buffet tables, and the dance floor. Add to these some of the less obvious, such as architectural features in the space, the doorways, windows, alcoves, and so forth.

Naturally, you must be selective. If everything is highlighted, the entire effect is lost. You end up with a bright, carnival atmosphere when what you really want is sweetness and magic. The contrast between dramatic highlights and the low, general lighting is what you must maintain. Try to envision the entire room when you plan the special effects. Balance the effects, spreading them around the walls and ceiling, so everybody will be surrounded with delightful visuals, both dim and bright.

The easiest and probably the most effective special lighting you can find is strings of tiny white Christmas tree lights. Lighting designers refer to these as fairy lights and use them with a lavish hand. Avoid the strings with multicolor bulbs; you want wedding magic, not Joyeux Noel.

Paul Mathiesen suggests you buy the fairy lights out of season and by the gross so you'll have the abundance you'll need to create opulence. The fairy lights are charming and very low wattage; has any-

L I G H T I N G

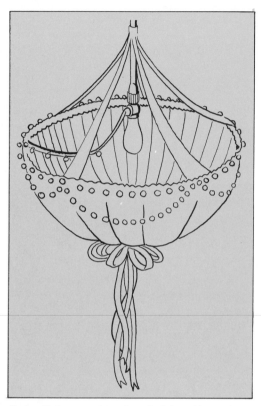

Fairy lights combined with fabric cover for light fixture

ing level from the modified overhead fixtures. No one has ever used too many strings of fairy lights.

Fairy lights also are good used in combination with the covers made to disguise tacky ceiling fixtures. Simply replace the bulb socket with one that has an extra female plug above the bulb. Plug the fairy lights into the socket and run them around the shade.

Paul Mathiesen suggests taking the fairy lights a step further and combining them with yards of tulle or netting in your wedding colors. Buy a whole bolt of tulle, which usually gets you a near-wholesale price. Bunch it up attractively and twine strings of fairy lights around the tulle. Trim with ribbons and drape it around windows and doorways.

The effect is fabulous, creating softened, magical entrances to step through. If you want some color variation in the fairy lights, dip some of the bulbs in thinned-out pink nail polish. The lights are cool enough and the tulle is porous enough so the combination is not dangerous. Ordinary household extension cords

one ever heard of a decorated Christmas tree blowing a circuit? They are made to be linked together, one end plugging into the next, so linking them in your party space needs no special effort or equipment.

Fairy lights are magical when used to highlight architectural features in an indoor space. Twine fairy lights around columns; use them to trace the curves of archways; frame fireplaces, windows, and doors with them. They can be taped in place or hung carefully with picture wire. Food service tables and bars can be outlined with fairy lights. The main thing is to use them with a free hand so you have many parts of the party space twinkling away, punctuating the general, low light-

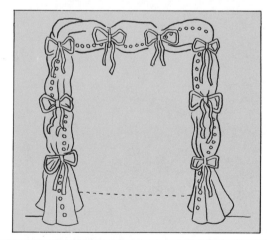

Doorway decorated with tulle and fairy lights

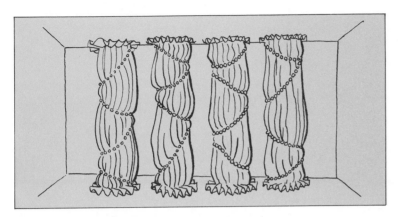

Light and tulle columns creating a focal point on a plain wall

can be used with fairy lights; remember to connect them to the power cord with the electrician's knot.

The Hermans recommend using fairy lights and tulle to create some architectural features in a boxy, boring room. If you have no fireplace, arches, and so on, you can establish focal points by loosely twisting tulle and fairy lights into floor-to-ceiling columns, spacing them along any long, plain wall. Use the placement to draw the guests' attention to the wall, perhaps behind the bridal table or the buffet tables.

Fairy lights, with or without tulle, work just as wonderfully outdoors as in. Use them to decorate your tent or fly; wind them around trees and bushes; drape serving tables; outline the exterior of nearby buildings and walkways. Again, the point is to use them in masses; just a few strands spread over a large area will have minimal impact.

You can achieve another dramatic effect by selecting three or four special objects or spaces and lighting them from below. (This is *very* dramatic so don't overdo it.) For example, if you place lighting fixtures on the floor (called "top hat" fixtures; see below for more details)

or ground directly beneath trees or tall floral arrangements, they will shoot light up through the greenery and cast leafy shadows on nearby walls or ceiling. Shadows from household ficus trees, indoor palms, or even big bunches of rhododendron leaves will work wonders against a light-colored wall or in an alcove. Cover the lights on the floor with lavender gels to enhance the look.

Floor fixtures can also be used to wash a larger area with light. For example, the wall of greenery described in the chapter on decor is perfect for floor lighting. "Top hat" fixtures are not frightfully expensive to purchase, but a homemade equivalent is just as effective and simple to make.

The homemade top hat fixtures are based on number 10 tin cans, that is, large tomato juice cans or the big, tall coffee cans. The can provides the housing for the socket and light bulb. For each top hat fixture you will need:

One number 10 can
One light socket (see illustration)
One R-40 or R-30 spotlight bulb, 75 watts
Plastic electrician's tape, not friction tape

Zip Cord in an appropriate gauge, enough to get where you're going, that is, the outlet

One male plug

Household extension cord, if needed

There are a number of light sockets on the market, but only one design is usable here. Since a metal can is the base, the socket must be made so that no bare wires touch the can. Electrical supply houses generally refer to this as a "two-piece cleat porcelain receptacle." Be sure you get sockets that look like this:

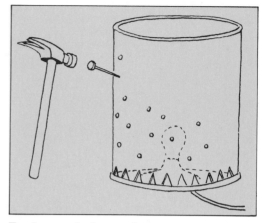

Top hat made from a #10 can

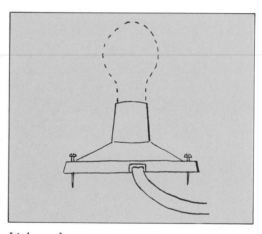

Light socket

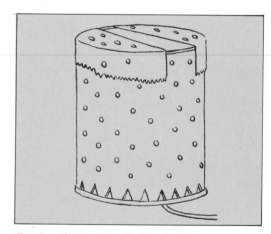

Top hat fixture masked with foil

Begin by drilling or hammering holes in the bottom of the can so the socket can be screwed firmly in place. Also make a hole on the lower side of the can to run the wire out, filing or taping the hole edge smooth so the wire insulation will not be damaged. Finally, make a dozen or so random holes in the can to help vent the heat buildup caused by the light bulb.

Open one end of the Zip Cord, remove an inch of the insulation, separate the two wires, and attach an end to each of the socket connections. Wrap the wire in the same direction the screw turns so the wire

will tighten as the connection is turned. Run the other end of the Zip Cord out the side hole you have prepared for it.

Match the bottom screw holes on the socket with those you made in the can bottom. Screw the socket firmly in place.

Wire the male plug onto the end of the Zip Cord, screw the spotlight bulb in, and your fixture is assembled. Plug into an outlet or an extension cord and play with the floor placement, moving the light around the tree or floral arrangement until you get the most pleasing shadows. The best effect depends on tight control of the beam of light. If it spills out all over the place, lighting up walls surrounding the alcove, you need to mask the top rim of the can with household aluminum foil.

There are several ways to mask off light. You can cut a 6-inch strip of foil, wind it around the top edge of the can, tape or wire it in place, and bend it in a cone shape, cutting down the diameter of the opening the light escapes through. Play with the foil until you get the light placement you want. Another way to mask the light is to run parallel strips of foil across the top of the can, boxing the opening with foil. Adjust the strips to get the boxed opening that will give you the light spill you want.

Top hat fixtures can be covered with gels. Be sure to make plenty of pinholes in the gel to help get rid of the heat buildup from the spotlight! The gels can be fastened on with gaffer's tape.

If you have limited space between the light fixture and the greenery, you may not need the special spotlight fixtures that work best at least 3 inches away from the greens. For example, wall niches or alcoves are super to use for lighting from below, but fixture placement can be a problem. Ask your hardware store people for suggestions, or experiment with regular 60- or 75-watt household bulbs and the foil cone mask to see if you can get an effect you like.

A hanging version of the top hat fixture is perfect to use over any areas in your party space that you want to spotlight, for example, the buffet table, bride's table, and dance floor.

If you can borrow any track lighting strips, you have your spotlight with no further effort, other than hanging them.

Home improvement centers sell 4-foot sections of track that come with several clip-on spotlights, ready to plug into any power outlet. Attach the track strip to a 4-foot batten (a pole, pipe, or piece of board will do) and hang the batten near the ceiling with wire and ceiling hooks. Tape the power cord to the suspension wire and across the ceiling to the nearest incandescent ceiling fixture. Buy a screw-in outlet socket, put it into a bulb socket, and plug the track lights into the fixture.

If track lights are not available, you may have access to the small clip-on light fixtures or can fixtures people use in bedrooms and dens. Check the wattage recommendations on the fixture; many of them can't take more than 60 watts. Suspend them the same way you would a track strip and run them off ceiling fixtures or extend the wires down to wall outlets. Track, clip-on, and can lights all can be gelled and masked with foil; they work well with tinted light bulbs as well as spotlights.

To make your own hanging spotlights follow the directions above for top hat fixtures but run the Zip Cord out of a hole you make in the bottom of the can rather than on the side. Cut venting holes with a beer can opener around the bottom of the can and increase the number of nail holes you make in the sides of the can. Hot air rises, so be sure it doesn't get trapped in the top of the number 10 can. To hang, suspend from a batten or direct from a cup hook placed in the ceiling.

Tom and Laura Herman suggest an alternative for hanging lights if you are not allowed to screw hooks into the ceiling. Most ceiling fixtures can be dropped down from the ceiling by simply unscrewing a

LIGHTING

*Track light on a beam
wired to a ceiling
light fixture*

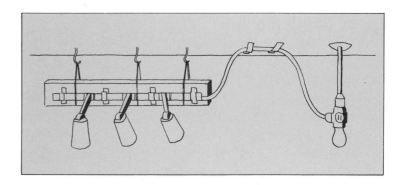

few screws. The Hermans drop a ceiling fixture down to get access to the hole in the ceiling above the fixture. They cut a small scrap of wood and fit it inside the opening, balancing it on top of the opening. The wood serves as a base to hang things from and is almost invisible when the fixture cap is taped up near the ceiling. Use a screw-in outlet in a bulb socket on the fixture for your power source.

▲▲▲▲▲▲▲

CANDLES

▼▼▼▼▼▼▼

Candles are the final part of your lighting design, adding a pretty glow to the general, low lighting and the special-effect fairy lights and spotlights. Everybody adores candles, and they are relatively inexpensive, so prepare to use them lavishly.

Mass small votive candles on the guests' tables. Votive candles really have to be in small glass containers; little juice or whisky glasses bought by the dozen hold them perfectly. Votive candles can also be worked into floral basket centerpieces or used to frame each table setting. They are also marvelously effective lined up on windowsills, mantles, wall shelves,

or alcoves. Just use lots of them and you won't go wrong!

A special outdoor use for votive candles comes to us from Mexico, where candles are used to decorate buildings during fiestas. Fill small paper bags with dirt or sand and turn over the tops a few times to get a stable collar. Place a votive candle in each bag, centering it in the sand. Line walkways with the bags and outline rooftops, porches, driveways, planting areas, and so forth. When lighted, the bag candles produce a soft, pretty glow. When the candles burn down, the wax runs into the sand, and the candle is self-extinguishing. Caution: Do not use to outline dance floors!

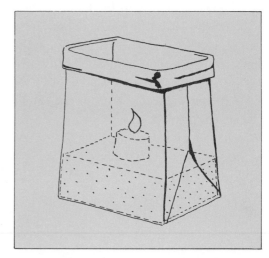

Paper bag lantern

The bride's table usually can use some large candelabra, either borrowed or rented, with very tall tapers in them. If nobody you know owns dramatic, Liberace-type candleholders, check local party rental companies for prices. Get them tall enough so nobody's vision is blocked; everybody wants to look at the bride and groom during the reception!

▲▲▲▲▲▲▲

PROFESSIONAL EQUIPMENT

▼▼▼▼▼▼▼

Professional stage lighting equipment is available for rent in almost every part of the country. Consider it only if your wedding is going to be very large and your plans call for very elaborate staging. There are problems with pro rentals: They are heavy-duty and must be used with heavy cables, booms, and stands. They really have to be run by professionals to be optimally effective. But if you are determined to use a follow spot, check your local high school, college, or little theater group to find the equipment to rent and somebody who is trained to handle it.

The only rental equipment that is fun and feasible for non-pro use is the motorized mirrored ball of 1920s ballroom fame, along with the tiny spotlights that give the mirror its sparkle. (Regular track lights or the homemade top hat fixtures won't be effective with a mirrored ball.) These low-voltage spotlights, called Rain Lights, throw a very narrow beam of intense light. They are trained on the revolving ball, and tiny squares of light are reflected, racing around the walls and ceiling of the party space as the mirror turns. The effect is terrific, and the cost is usually modest.

Check local theatrical supply houses, lighting stores, and local headshops—mirrored balls were an underground sensation during the 1960s. If you can locate one, the renter will give you directions for installation and will probably furnish the Rain Lights also.

Obviously there are a zillion ways to light a party space. All you have to do is let your imagination soar! When asked for a few words of summary, Paul, Laura, Tom, and Greg came up with similar statements:

- Keep your plan as simple as possible.
- Try to use borrowed or homemade equipment.
- Keep the end result in mind; don't get overinvolved in the equipment so you forget the point of the event.
- Make sure the lighting transforms the space completely.
- *Think magic.*

▼ *The Lighting worksheets can be found on pages 212–13.*

LIGHTING

▲▲▲▲▲▲▲

DECOR AND PROPS

▼▼▼▼▼▼▼

11

DECOR AND PROPS

T his chapter is divided into two sections; the first explores the possibilities for decorating the party space you have selected, and the second covers the "how-to" for making the props you might need for the wedding. The word "prop" is a shortened form of the word property, which the Oxford American Dictionary defines as "a movable object used on stage during a performance of a play," and so forth. For our purposes, the wedding props include the ring bearer's pillow, the decorated cake knife, the chupah, food carts, fabric roses, and the bachelor party cake.

▲▲▲▲▲▲▲▲

WEDDING DECOR

▽▽▽▽▽▽▽

Interior designer Barnett Simons tells us, "Right from the start, party decorating is fun. You want to make your space stand out and be noticed, reflecting the point of view you've chosen for the celebration. This is where the fantasy comes in. Rule of thumb: Your party space should never look like home!

"First, decide on the colors. Go through your fabric boards and pick out one dominant color for major use and one backup color that can be added in. The colors can be two different shades of one hue, say deep apricot and pale peach, or can be true contrasts if you like.

"Then take your colors in hand and visit the party space. Look objectively at the room. You have to base your decorating on transforming that room into what you want it to be. You already have established a concept for the wedding, so review that again, this time with decorating in mind."

Every decor needs a focal point. Sometimes you'll be lucky enough to get a space with a wonderful focal point: a grand fireplace, a bank of windows, a raised area with architectural interest. If so, your decorating problems are minimal and can be centered around the focal point, making the most of it with greenery, flowers, and lighting. Do whatever you can to draw people's eyes to the focal point. A terrific looking fireplace can be banked with greenery, flowers, and ribbons, topped with tall, lighted tapers, and perhaps flanked with indoor trees or tall floral arrangements lighted from below. (See the chapter on lighting.)

Make your focal point rather theatrical and light it so that it stands out above the general, low illumination in the rest of the space. Masses of candles are great to use on and around the focal point. Or consider the fairy lights and tulle described in the chapter on lighting.

Whatever effects you choose must be done lavishly, or they will be lost on your guests. More is better for party decorations. Remember that the room will be filled with people all dressed up and excited. If the decor is too subtle it will be lost in the drama of the party rather than contributing to the festiveness.

Unfortunately, rooms with great, built-in focal points are more the exception than the rule. Most rental halls are rather dreary, rectangular spaces. Too many have imitation dark wood paneling, well suited to a meeting of the Rotary but pretty bad for a wedding of sweetness and light.

If your party space is less than wonderful, you'll need to do something radical. Barnett suggests an inexpensive, fabulously effective way to create a focal point: Make a leafy bower by covering a large portion of one wall from floor to ceiling with greenery. Once constructed, the bower should be treated as a built-in architectural feature, lighting and decorating it so it becomes a standout. The bower can be made and hung the day before the party, provided the greenery you choose will not wilt overnight.

This bower is based on chicken wire with greens woven through the openings. Select the wall you want to use as your focal point and pace off the amount of space you want to cover with the bower. Try to figure at least 6 feet to 8 feet wide from floor to ceiling. Anything much smaller will look like a silly stripe of green running down one wall. You want a bower with impact! Sketch the bower in on your floor plan and consider where you will attach it to the wall/ceiling and what power outlets are nearby for the lighting.

DECOR AND PROPS

Once you have your measurements, buy two battens, one for the bower top and one for the bottom. A batten can be a board 1 foot by 3 feet, or any rigid support that can be hung at the top of the wall near the ceiling. Then buy enough chicken wire to cover the wall area from floor to ceiling. Staple, wire, or nail the chicken wire onto the battens to form a base for the greenery.

Cut or purchase large amounts of laurel leaves, smilax, pine, evergreen, or other leafy branches that will not wilt without water. Laurel is especially durable and grows abundantly in many parts of the United States. Laurel is perfect for this project since it grows in four- or five-leaf clusters that can be inserted into the chicken wire to form an overall green panel. The leaf clusters will be much easier to control if you keep them small.

The amount of greenery needed depends on the width and height of your bower. You need to pack the branches rather closely onto the chicken wire, so be prepared to use a lot of greenery.

Suspend the batten and chicken wire framework in the selected spot on the wall, making sure it is firmly in place and can hold the weight of the branches. Once it is up you can begin weaving leafy clusters into the wire, using fine craft or florist wire to secure anything that looks precarious. Work from the top down, getting dense coverage so no wall peeks through.

Once the basic bower is in place there are many ways to decorate it. Think about lighting first; fairy lights woven into the leaves are an option. Or add glitz by spray glueing portions of the greenery and tossing sparkle dust onto the wet spray, work-

Greenery wall covering based on a frame of chicken wire and batten

ing for an overall light sprinkle of glitter. Then make a few top hat fixtures and light either from above or below.

Other charming additions to the bower are ribbons, bows, and streamers all over the greenery. Woven ribbons are expensive to use in massive amounts, and the success of the decorating depends on lavish use. Buy three or four-yard lengths of pretty print or solid fabrics in your colors, and cut the fabric into ribbon-sized strips. The effect will be the same, and you'll save money.

Use the directions for the florist's bow in Chapter 8, Flowers, and make sizable rosettes with streamers, with knotted and braided narrow ribbons coming down from them. Artificial flowers can be used to ac-

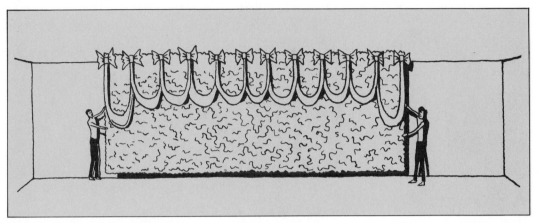

Leafy bower draped with ribbons

cent the greenery as long as they are rather large in scale. Tiny blossoms will become almost invisible against a wall of greens. All decorations must be in your colors and must relate to the overall look of the wedding.

If fresh flowers are available, you can decorate the bower with individual large blossoms. Live flowers need water, so the bower must be set up to hold small glass tubes wired in place and filled with water. The tubes are standard florist's equipment, come in several sizes, and are inexpensive. Check florist supply houses or order through a local florist. Tubes can also be made from the plastic cases toothbrushes come in or from science class test tubes. Spot the flowers in the greenery and back them up with lots of ribbons and streamers.

A pretty way to tie the bower into the rest of the room is to make garlands from the same greenery and festoon them around the top of the other walls. See garland making directions in the chapter on flowers.

Occasionally a rented space with a very high ceiling has an airplane hangar feeling. Barnett recommends visually elimi-

nating the height with a series of large banners suspended from the ceiling, spaced across the width of the room. Work in your wedding colors, adding a third shade to achieve a heraldic look to your banners.

Ceiling banners don't have to be made of fabric. Very wide butcher's paper can serve as a base, with color-coordinated crepe paper or tissue paper spray glued on to create the patterns. If plain fabrics such as old white sheets are available, use those as banner bases. There is no need to hem the sides and bottom, just

Garlands wrapped with ribbon

DECOR AND PROPS

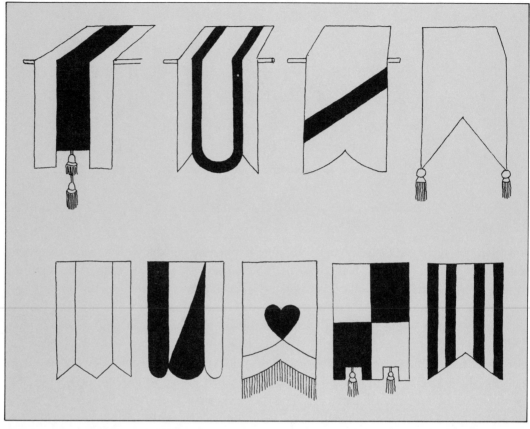

Ceiling banners

cut the edges straight and be sure no threads hang down.

Work with your floor plan to estimate the size and number of banners you'll need. Use them lavishly, as you will all the other decorative elements. Sketch them in across the room, noting where they can be suspended, from the side of the room or from the ceiling fixtures. Plan your banners to be at least 3 feet wide and about 5 feet long. A traditional medieval banner bottom is fishtailed, that is, cut up to a point in the center.

The patterns you choose can be heraldic in inspiration or can go in any direction that pleases you. Patterns have to be large scale; small figures and detailing

will be lost as soon as the banners are hung. Barnett offered a few sketches for reference (above).

To fabricate, get one batten per banner; any rigid material will do that won't droop when hung. Put small eye screws on the batten ends to facilitate hanging. Glue or staple the banner base material onto the batten and lightly sketch your pattern in pencil. Fill in the pattern with paper, paint, whatever, making both sides of the banner identical. For extra decorating, make a 4-inch paper fringe and glue along the bottom and/or top. Attach streamers and ribbons if needed.

For a more delicate version of a banner use wide lengths of netting or cheese-

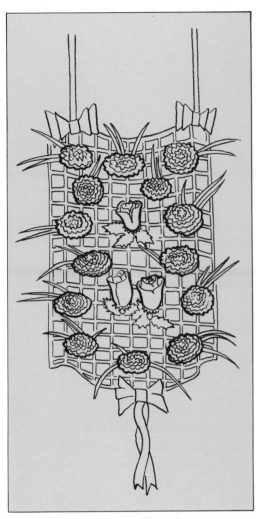

Netting and flower banner

cloth, with huge paper flowers attached and decorated with ribbons and streamers. Follow the directions at the end of this chapter for making paper flowers, but increase the size so that each flower is at least 1 foot across.

Paper banners might need to be weighted on the bottom to hang gracefully. You won't know this until you loft a few, so try them and see. An easy way to weight banners is to tape pennies onto the lower edge, hiding them with extra fringe, cords, or tassels. Hang all the banners at

approximately the same height, using either thin picture wire or nylon fishing line. Or use wide ribbons and streamers, making a decorative element of the hanging apparatus.

If a bower is not allowed on the walls of your space, free-hanging canopies can be suspended from the ceiling to create charming focal points over the bride's table, the buffet table, the dance floor, and so forth. Build a very light framework of rigid material the size of the table or area you want to highlight. Lash together rigid plastic tubing or thin strips of wooden lathe to form a rectangle, and run thin wire across to fill in the open space.

Cover the framework with branches of laurel, smilax, or other long-lasting leaves, wired on and held in place with pretty ribbons. Make the garland full and lush, and then begin to decorate the greenery with ribbons, bows, streamers, artificial or real flowers, fairy lights, and so on. (See diagram on next page.)

When a canopy is as decorated as you want it to be, suspend it from the ceiling directly over whatever area you want to highlight. Focus lights on the canopies so all eyes are drawn to them and away from the not-so-great walls and ceiling.

Table covers must be floor length, says Barnett Simons, and must relate to your wedding color scheme. If only white cloths are available from the linen rental company, add colored ribbons, flowers, napkins, and candles in your colors to tie everything together.

Runners of plain or printed fabric in your wedding colors can also be used, crisscrossed over the solid color tablecloths. These don't even have to be hemmed; merely cut long lengths of fabric

DECOR AND PROPS

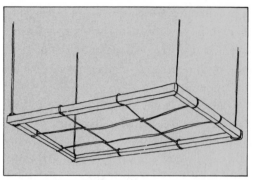

Frame for hanging canopy

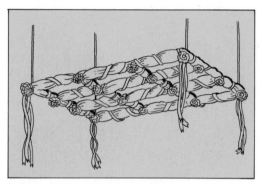

Decorated hanging canopy

and place them to form a pattern on the white cloth. Large fern fronds are another possibility to liven up a plain tablecloth. Simply fan them out from your table centerpiece on a round table, or make a line of them down the center of a rectangular table.

▲▲▲▲▲▲▲▲

MISCELLANEOUS PROPS

▽▽▽▽▽▽▽

A chupah must be constructed for a Jewish wedding. The chupah is the small canopy under which the bride and groom stand during the ceremony. It can be anything from a simple piece of fabric suspended on four poles carried by four friends to an elaborate free-standing floral piece reaching up and curving over the bridal party.

Many families have an heirloom that is used as the chupah. The tallith, or prayer shawl, that the groom wore at his bar mitzvah is often used, or any ceremonial piece of embroidery that has special meaning for either family.

If no meaningful fabric exists, you have carte blanche to create your own and can make it as fanciful as you like; or you can

be serious and start your own heirloom tradition. According to Helene Ferris, Associate Rabbi of the Stephen Wise Free Synagogue in New York City, the only restriction is that the chupah must shelter at least the bridal couple during the ceremony. Additional people may be placed under the chupah, however: the rabbi, the cantor, and/or the parents of the bride and groom.

In the make-your-own-heirloom category, embroidered panels done by close friends and relatives are a wonderfully loving gift to the bride and groom. Each needleworker adds her own graphic good wish for the couple, illustrated perhaps with appliqué or other embellishment. Printed, painted, or stenciled panels are great alternatives. Sew small triangles of fabric on the four corners to facilitate attaching to the poles.

A version of the hanging canopy described earlier in this chapter can become the chupah when filled with gathered tulle or netting and attached to four poles. Or, if the ceremony is to be in the same space as the reception, a marquee extension can be added to the wall bower, reaching out far enough to shelter the couple.

A freestanding floral chupah can be constructed from a lawn trellis kit avail-

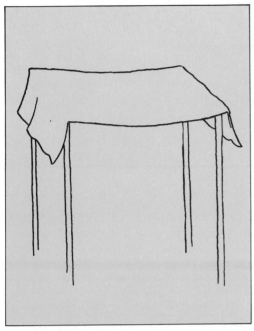

Fabric chupah

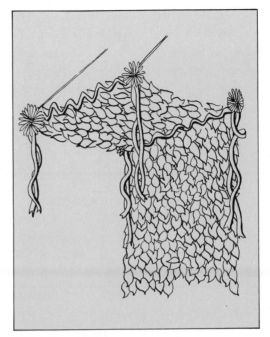

Chupah marquee

Trellis chupah

DECOR AND PROPS

able at home improvement centers. Several styles of trellises are available in kit form or in sectional units. Choose the arched one or sections that can be connected into an arch. The trellis arch is put in place before any guests arrive; it is not carried on poles by attendants. Build a wooden base so the arch stands securely and spray paint the whole thing in your wedding color.

Once painted, weave and wire greenery onto the trellis and decorate with any or all of the items suggested in the directions for the wall bower. The greenery can be done the day before, and the fresh flowers, in their little water tubes, added a few hours before the ceremony.

Service carts are alternatives to buffet tables for food service; often they can be rented from party rental services. The carts look like tea wagons and can be decorated with greenery, fabrics, ribbons, bows, and flowers. Carts work well indoors or out, and are a simple yet festive way to make your space usage more flexible. Just wheel them out of the way when the dancing begins.

The hand props (the ring bearer's pillow, the bride's garter, and the wedding cake cutter) become charming objects when coordinated with bridal attire. Fabric roses and rosebuds can facilitate the coordination and are astonishingly simple to make. Our instructions come from Ellen Hannan Delgado, who was taught fabric rose making in the third grade at St. Joseph Hill Academy on Staten Island. The instructions sound confusing but make sense if you follow them step by step, with a ribbon strip in hand.

The fabric rose is based on a ribbon or cut strip of fabric at least 1 yard long.

Fold the strip in half and then slide one side of the fold down to make a 45-degree-angle fold.

Hold the diagonal fold with thumb and forefinger, and stretch the ribbon ends out on a flat surface. Then, alternating ends of ribbon, begin folding up and over the triangle, laying the ribbon end out on the flat surface. Do not let go of the diagonal fold triangle.

When the ribbon is completely folded, run a fingernail over the creases, setting them in. Then hold the two ribbon ends between thumb and forefinger and release the folded section.

Still holding tight, gently pull the bottom ribbon end toward you. Keep pulling slowly and evenly as the creased ribbon bunches up into "petals" held in place by the pressure of thumb and forefinger. When you get the fullness you like, either knot or stitch the ribbon ends together, or wrap with florist's wire or a twist tie to keep the flower together.

The size of the rose depends on the length and width of your fabric strip or ribbon, from adorable little rosebuds to big, lush blossoms. Large or small, they all combine well with artificial leaves from a millinery supply or craft supply store. Use them lavishly on all your hand props!

The ring bearer's pillow can be any small baby or doll carriage pillow, covered in white or one of your wedding fabrics. Lace edging is often stitched around the edges, with fabric roses and ribbon streamers on the corners. A 12-inch piece of narrow ribbon is folded in half and the fold point sewn onto the middle of the covered pillow so the ring(s) can be tied in place with a pretty bow. If your ring

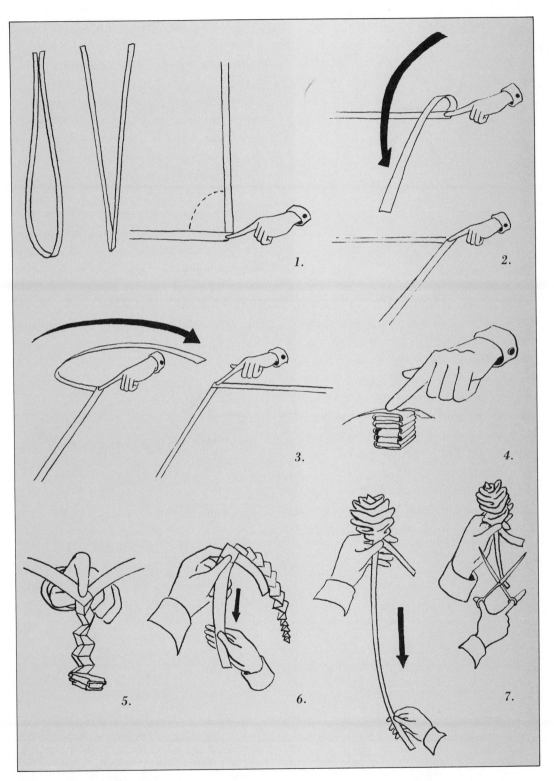

How to Make a Fabric Rose

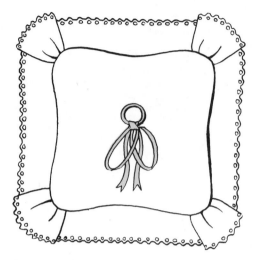

Ring bearer's pillow

bearer is very young, you might want to stitch two ribbon loops on the underside of the pillow for him to slide his hands into so there's no worry about dropping the pillow.

The cutting of the wedding cake is a major ceremonial part of the reception, so be sure to make a decorative delight out of your cake knife. An inexpensive, long cutting knife is fine for the base. If the handle is wood, spray paint it with your wedding color or spray glue it and cover with wrapped ribbon or fabric. It should never look like something from the kitchen!

Decorated cake knife

Decorate the knife with fabric rosebuds, ribbons, lace, or streamers to give it the same feeling as the bridal bouquets. Tie, tape, staple, or wire the decorations where the cutting blade joins the handle. When the time comes to present the wedding cake, have the decorated knife on the tray, ready to be used.

The bride's garter is another prop that is fun to make. Begin with a 1-inch-wide strip of elastic, long enough to fit comfortably below the bride's knee. Make a fabric casing in white or in a wedding fabric long enough to cover the elastic when it is stretched out as far as it can go. Topstitch narrow lace edging onto the casing. Slide the elastic into the casing and sew the ends together.

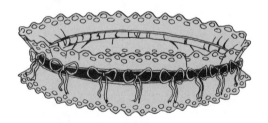

Bride's garter

Ask the bride to wear the garter for a few hours before decorating it to see if it is tight enough to stay in place and yet loose enough so circulation is not stopped. Make tiny rosebuds, bows, and so forth and sew them over the seam that joins the casing. Keep the decorations small and flat so the garter won't form a lump under the wedding gown.

The final prop in this chapter is not for the wedding or reception—it's the large cardboard cake for the bachelor party referred to in Chapter 4, Protocol. New York scenic artist Jill Tannone worked with us to design an incredible 45-inch-high cake. First, find a good sport who will agree to jump out of the cake. Then, to make one, you will need the following:

Large roll of 18-inch-high corrugated cardboard

Roll of 3-inch-wide gaffer's tape

Several rolls of household transparent tape

Exacto knife, scissors

2 plastic hula hoops

Old newspapers

2 or 3 large sheets of cardboard (3 feet by 4 feet)

6 to 8 cotton balls and bright red nail polish

spray glue

crepe paper in your "cake" colors, that is, white with one or two accent colors, to cover the cake

4 or 5 packs of brightly colored tissue paper

2 yards of wide ribbon in the cake's accent color

1 very large cardboard box, the kind major appliances are shipped in— large enough to hold a squatting person

1) Cut the appliance box so it measures 18 inches high. Place the box, cut side up, on top of sheets of cardboard.

2) Tape the cardboard sheets together to form one surface. Then sketch a circle on the cardboard, spacing it so it fills in the corners of the box and makes a cake-like circle.

3) Cut out the circle and tape a length of corrugated cardboard around it, to form a cake layer. For stability, cut strips of cardboard and fold them into braces, tap-

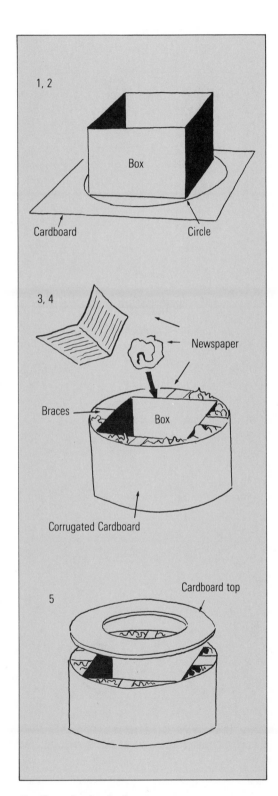

Cardboard cake, 1–5

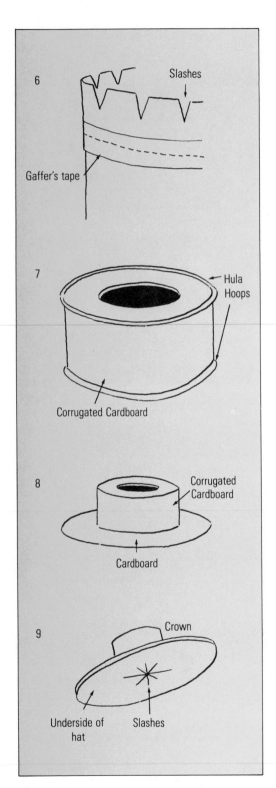

Cardboard cake, 6–9

ing them from the cut edge of the box down into the corrugated cardboard.

4) Stuff crumpled newspapers between the box and the corrugated cardboard for extra solidity.

5) Piece together a cardboard doughnut to be used as the top of the first cake layer. You will want it to meet the corrugated cardboard circle edge rather exactly and to overhang the cut box edge a small amount so the second layer of the cake can rest on it.

6) To attach, run a strip of gaffer's tape around the corrugated cardboard, spacing it so the lower half of the tape is in contact with the cardboard. Slash the upper part of the tape every 3 inches or 4 inches and fold it smoothly over the doughnut to hold it in place.

7) For the second layer, tape corrugated cardboard in a circle around one of the hula hoops. Reinforce the joining with slashed gaffer's tape so it all looks relatively smooth. When it feels sturdy, place the second hula hoop in the other end of the corrugated cardboard circle and tape it in place. Set it aside; do not attach to the bottom cake layer.

8) The third layer is the hat the jumping person will wear. Make a cardboard circle just big enough to sit on top of the hula hoop layer. Cut a strip of corrugated cardboard in half horizontally so it's about 9 inches high. Form it into a circle about 13 inches in diameter and tape it in the middle of the third circle of cardboard to form the crown. Fill in the top with more cardboard and tape in place, using the slashed gaffer's tape method to get smooth joinings.

9) Estimate the approximate center of the hat brim circle. Working from underneath, make a small hole in the center of the circle. Make cuts with the Exacto knife, running in a sunburst from the center out to where the crown joins the brim. Gently push the triangular cuts up a little so the wearer's head can fit into the crown and the hat will stay on her head.

10) Using the spray glue, cover the entire cake, layer by layer. Work your way around the cake, spraying a vertical strip and smoothing the paper in place. Cover the underside of the brim on the hat layer since it will be visible to the guests.

11) Make four or six candles from the other 9-inch strip of corrugated cardboard, tightly rolling 5-inch widths and taping them into candle shapes.

12) Spray glue each candle and cover it with colored paper. Cut small X's around the hat brim where you want to place the candles. Gently push the candles up into the X cuts and tape them securely in place. Top each candle with a cotton ball twisted into a flame shape and dipped in red nail polish.

13) Cut two thin openings on each side of the hat brim and insert 1 yard of tie ribbon on each side so the hat can be tied in place.

14) Begin decorating the bottom layer of the cake. Festoon twisted strips of crepe paper around the layer and tape in place. Make big fantasy flowers from the colored tissue paper and tape the blossoms on, spacing them so that they hold the hula hoop layer in place.

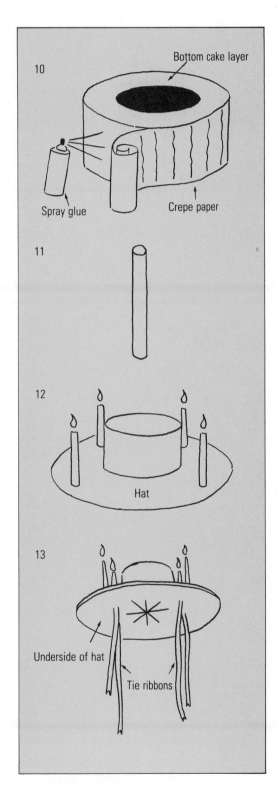

Cardboard cake, 10–13

DECOR AND PROPS

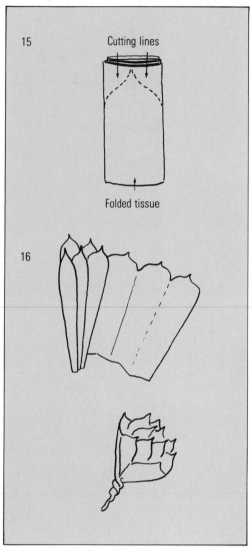

Making paper flowers, 15–16

15) To make tissue flowers, cut strips of tissue about 7 inches wide and accordion-fold together two contrasting color strips to make a packet about 3 inches wide. Trim a petal shape onto one end.

16) Open the packet out and begin rolling and gathering the papers to form a flower. Gently fan the petals for fullness. Tape the bottom of the flower to keep it together, and then tape it onto the cake.

17) To assemble, put the bottom layer on a dolly or movable cart, and a small stool in the bottom of the box. Have the person who will jump get into the box and sit. Slide the hula hoop layer over the person and place it within the taped circle of flowers on the bottom layer. Tie on the hat to complete the assemblage. Present the cake with appropriate music.

Cake in action, 17

▼ *The Decor and Props worksheet can be found on pages 214–15.*

12

▲▲▲▲▲▲▲

BEVERAGE
SERVICE

▼▼▼▼▼▼▼

▼▼▼▼▼▼

▼ ▼ ▼ ▼ ▼ ▼

F or centuries humans have been sharing a ceremonial beverage to commemorate an event or seal a pact. Drinking a toast to the bride and groom is a charming part of that heritage. Envision a room full of smiling people raising their glasses to the newlyweds. The toast symbolizes every wish for a wonderful future, so make sure the beverage service at your reception is handled graciously and hospitably.

Use the workbook pages for beverage service as a planning guide and shopping list, and for on-site reference. Photocopy the pages after you've filled them in and give each of your volunteers a set so everybody has the same information to work with.

▲▲▲▲▲▲▲

ESTIMATING QUANTITIES AND PLANNING YOUR PURCHASES

▼▼▼▼▼▼▼

Since your guests will have varied needs and tastes, the first step is to divide them into workable categories in order to plan beverages. The first grouping is by age. Estimate as well as you can. If you are having 150 people to the reception, your age groupings might look like this:

Age	Number of People
Under 18 years	20
Between 18 and 30	50
Between 30 and 60	50
Over 60	30

Next, accumulate data on beverage preferences for each group. You know the under-eighteens are going to be served nonalcoholic beverages. Do some research and find out what will make your twenty under-eighteen guests happiest— a sparkly punch, brand name or generic soft drinks, fruit juices, and so forth. Make a list of all possibilities.

The eighteen to thirty group is probably your contemporaries, and you already know what they like to drink. Write down the choices, including the brand names of beers, wines, and hard liquors. Add information about coffee and tea drinking so you can be relatively accurate about tastes for after-meal beverages.

Your parents will be the source of information for the last two categories. They know what their friends and relatives like to be served and what they'll feel comfort-

able with. There will be people who don't drink alcohol, so find out what the non-liquor-drinking guests will enjoy. Add tea, coffee, and decaffeinated coffee data to your list.

Next, you need to decide for how long each of the various kinds of beverages is going to be served. For example, you might decide to have the following:

Receiving line/cocktails: from 4 to 5:15 P.M.

Food/wine/coffee service: from 5:15 to 7 P.M.

Dancing/open bar: from 7 to 8:15 P.M.

Wedding cake presentation: 8:15 P.M.

Bridal couple leaves reception: 9:30 P.M.

Your budget will tell you how much money you have allocated to beverages. Your shopping must be based on the budget figure; the point to all money management is to spread the available money around so it buys what needs to be bought. Fortunately, there are many alternatives to consider.

Stephen J. Churchville, bar manager of New York City's elegant Bridge Cafe, offers some ground rules. "You can safely estimate two to three drinks per adult for the first hour and one to two drinks per adult per hour after that. Children drink more, so plan on three sodas per person per hour. If you want to serve wine with dinner, figure between one and two glasses per adult.

"Make life easier by standardizing glass sizes. Use 4-to-5-ounce cups for wine and eight-ounce cups for everything else except the champagne. The disposable, clear-plastic cups are handy since guests need a fresh cup with each drink

BEVERAGE SERVICE

during cocktail hour. People will refill wineglasses when they're seated at tables during dinner. Plan on five to six cups per person, and have a few spare packages for backup.

"Then there are some things everybody knows: Mixed drinks are the most expensive to serve. Generic or house brands cost less than nationally advertised brands. Domestic brands cost less than imports. Punches, beers, and wines cost less than mixed drinks. Keg beer costs less than canned beer. Jug wines cost less than bottles. Large bottles of soda cost less than cans. Inexpensive champagne is fine for the bridal toast since it's poured in advance and the glasses are passed to guests and nobody sees the labels.

"A quart of liquor is 32 ounces; a good bar drink contains between 1½ and 2 ounces, plus mix, ice, and garnish. You can figure around sixteen drinks per bottle."

Steve recommends simplifying the liquor list if you decide to serve mixed drinks. Look over the drink preferences of your guests and try to select the four or five kinds of hard liquor everybody will drink. "Today people usually drink more white liquor than brown liquor. Vodka leads the list; people drink vodka two to one over scotch, rye, and bourbon. Actually, people drink vodka two to one over gin also."

Your mixed drink list might be vodka, scotch, bourbon, and gin. To serve martinis and manhattans, add to the list sweet and dry vermouth.

Unless your beer-drinking guests have fanatic loyalty to one certain canned beer, you'll be smart to serve keg beer. Kegs of local, national, and imported beer come in three sizes: quarter kegs (7½ gallons), half kegs (15 gallons), and full kegs (30 gallons).

Bartender Felito de Narvaez, whose credits include designing and setting up the beverage service for New York's trendy Kamikaze Klub and BeBop Cafe, recommends quarter kegs. "Even though you can serve up to fifty people per full keg, a whole keg is unwieldy. Quarter kegs are easy to move around and can be stored in 30-gallon plastic garbage cans packed with ice.

"Order the quarter kegs to be delivered cold, several hours before the party begins. Stack them and cover with a tarpaulin to keep in the cold. Buy two 30-gallon plastic garbage cans, pack some unopened bags of ice in each, slide in a quarter keg, and top with more bags of ice. Serve beer from one and have the second waiting as a backup. When a quarter keg is finished, replace it in the garbage can with a full one, which will have time to rechill while you serve the backup.

"If you've never tapped a keg of beer, ask your beer supplier for directions. It's easy to do and takes only a minute. A professional bartender will tap several kegs each evening."

Wine drinkers echo the white-over-color preferences of the liquor drinkers. Purchase two-thirds of your wine total white and the other one-third red. The white wine should be delivered chilled several hours before the party. Then pack bottles or jugs of white wine in plastic garbage cans filled with unopened bags of ice. Red wine is served at room temperature and will benefit from standing un-corked for forty-five minutes before serving. You may simplify wine service by placing opened bottles of wine on each dining table. The reds may be put out early, during the setup before the party. The whites, chilled, can be put on the tables just as the guests are going through the buffet line.

Consider serving punches instead of mixed drinks during the cocktail hour. Historically, warm and cold punches were served regularly for important occasions. In Colonial America silversmiths like Paul Revere created beautiful punch ser-vices that are now in major museums. Today the advantages of punches are many: They are festive, simplify the bev-erage service, cost much less than mixed drinks, and can be as potent or as nonal-coholic as you see fit.

Recipes are in most cookbooks and in bartender's guides. A champagne punch or a sangria looks marvelous and is totally appropriate; hot mulled cider or glögg can brighten up a cold weather reception. Test small quantities of all punch recipes that sound good so you're sure of the taste and you've had a little experience making them. Never take a chance by serving an untried, untasted punch!

Punch bowls and ladles can be rented from party rental companies. Serve a summer punch bowl resting on a bed of ice. Avoid using blocks of ice in a punch since ice melts and waters down the bev-erage. Replace ice blocks with frozen fruit juices or other nonalcoholic ingredients, prettied up with fruits and garnishes fro-zen in. Or freeze layers of different juices in one container for a rainbow effect. Do

this by freezing a layer of one juice, then adding a second juice over the solidly fro-zen first layer, and so on.

Serve a winter punch bowl over a Sterno burner or camp stove artfully dis-guised to fit into the table decorations. Heat will release all the enticing spice aromas to greet your guests.

When estimating quantities of punch, plan on 4-ounce servings per person and total the ounces of ingredients. For exam-ple, if seventy-five guests will be served sangria in 4-ounce cups, each round of drinks will require 300 ounces of sangria. If each person drinks three cups, you'll need to provide at least 900 ounces. You therefore should make over 7 gallons of sangria, with a little extra in case it's so fabulous everyone clamors for more!

Use the same method to estimate the amount of soda and/or fruit juices you'll need for the nondrinkers and the chil-dren. First decide which sodas are most popular among your guests. Probably your list would include seltzer or club soda, 7-Up or lemon/lime, cola, ginger ale, or-ange juice, and grape juice.

Use your research to help you decide how much of each to buy, proportionately. Multiply the cup/ounce size by the number of drinkers; then multiply by the number of cups you think each person will drink. Get the total of ounces needed and divide that into the soda bottle sizes you intend to purchase. (With the metric system encroaching, bear in mind that a liter equals 33.8 fluid ounces and 1.75 liters equals 59.7 fluid ounces—roughly relating to a 32-ounce quart and a 64-ounce half gallon.)

Most of the above list will also meet

BEVERAGE SERVICE

your need for drink mixes, with the addition of tonic water, Tom Collins mix, and tomato juice.

Base your purchases on the preferences of your guests, and figure roughly 3 to 4 ounces of mix per drink.

Mixed drinks require garnishes such as limes, lemons, oranges, olives, onions, celery, and cherries.

"Use the bartender's cut for easy handling and a professional look," says Felito. "Cut each lime in half from end to end. Then cut the pieces from end to end again, and finally, quarter each piece. You'll end up with eight equal pieces that release their juices with a light squeeze.

"For lemons, you will need mostly twists, so trim off the tops and bottoms, outline ¼-inch strips with the tip of your paring knife, running the length of the lemon. Push a spoon down between the peel and the pulp, freeing the strips. Separate the ¼-inch strips and cut each one into 1-inch lengths. Offer the lemon pulp to the kitchen staff for cooking purposes.

"For a party of one hundred fifty people I'd buy twenty limes, ten to twelve lemons, one package of celery, and one bottle each of olives and onions. I'd leave two or three lemons unpeeled in case I needed a garnish for a Tom Collins."

Both Steve and Felito agree that ice is crucial to any party, and it is the trickiest commodity to estimate. Much depends on the weather and the serving conditions. "Ice cubes last longer if you keep them unopened in the plastic bags they come in," says Steve. "Pack unopened bags around beers and wines, and open them one at a time as you need cubes. Borrow Styrofoam picnic coolers and store bags in

Have you ever wondered how the pros manage to get all the champagne served for the bridal toast without a deafening barrage of cork poppings? Steve tells us the secret: "Put out all the glasses on serving trays long before the guests arrive. Then, right before the guests walk in, open all the champagne bottles but do not pour anything. Roll up two or three cocktail napkins to form a paper 'cork' and plug up the top of each bottle. This will hold the fizz for a couple of hours. Return the bottles to your coolers or place them over ice. When toast time arrives, all you have to do is pour, and the trays are ready to go."

His pro instructions for opening champagne bottles bear repeating: "Remove the wire cage. Hold the bottle away from your chest at about a 30-degree angle. Grip the cork tightly but do not push out the cork. Slowly twist the bottle and the cork in opposite directions. The cork will slide out with a gentle pop, and the champagne will not spill all over the place."

them to make sure you'll have ice all through the party."

When asked to estimate the amount of ice each would order for a five-hour wedding reception for one hundred fifty people, Felito said he'd get seventy-five pounds, and Steve opted for sixty to sixty-five pounds. However, both gentlemen recommended over-ordering on the ice, especially if volunteers are tending bar.

Steve and Felito also agreed that glasses should be rented for the champagne toast if at all possible. The toast is one of the highlights of the party and will be even more festive if real glasses are used. Plan on getting six and one half or seven glasses from each bottle of champagne.

▲▲▲▲▲▲▲

SETTING UP THE BAR

▼▼▼▼▼▼▼

The physical setup of a bar is especially important if the bartenders are not experienced professionals. One enthusiastic person can handle a fifty-person event smoothly, but once you get up to seventy-five guests you should recruit two volunteers or sets of two volunteers to bartend in shifts. A "bar boy" volunteer is needed even if a professional is behind the bar, to check in every half hour, refill water pitchers, bring extra supplies, and be generally helpful.

Two 6-foot tables paralleling each other are the ideal setup for a bar. The front table is the actual service table, and the back table is for storage. The bartenders stand between the tables, reaching back for the supplies to fill a drink order.

"Keep the booze away from people," Felito warns. "Place all liquor bottles in the center of the rear table and put all the glasses, garnishes, and supplies on each end. Place garbage cans of wine, beer, and ice under the rear table, within easy reach. Stack up Styrofoam coolers and extra kegs under the front table. Place the working beer keg so the spigot faces away from the guests, out of reach. Surround the back of the bar with trash containers, which the bar boy can empty every so often.

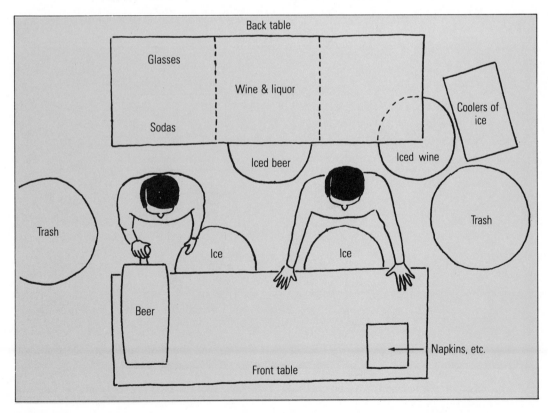

Two-table service bar

"If the front table has a Formica top, you'll be able to sponge it off and keep it clean. If not, cover with a tablecloth, and have several extra cloths stashed nearby so you can change the cover every hour or two as it gets soaked and messy. Put napkins, matches, ashtrays, and sipstirs on the front table."

If you have space for only one table, try to get a 6-foot Formica one, and use the space behind it on the floor to store ice-filled garbage cans and beer kegs. Surround the rear area with trash containers that are easily emptied by the bar boy but big enough to keep people from getting into the supplies. You want them standing in front of the bar.

Steve says, "For a one-table, two person setup, divide the beverage service into two parts. One bartender serves only mixed drinks, while the other serves wine, beer, and soda. Put open soda bottles in the middle of the table and keep an ice container on the floor between the two bartenders. Make sure everybody has everything within reach so each person can work efficiently and neither has to ever move away from the bar. If the bar is left untended, things get out of control."

Whether it's one table or two, a bar needs to be equipped with tools. Provide each bartender with the following:

1 small cutting board and paring knife
1 corkscrew
1 bottle opener
1 can opener
sponges
towels
bowl of water for cleanup
large, heavy-duty trash bags

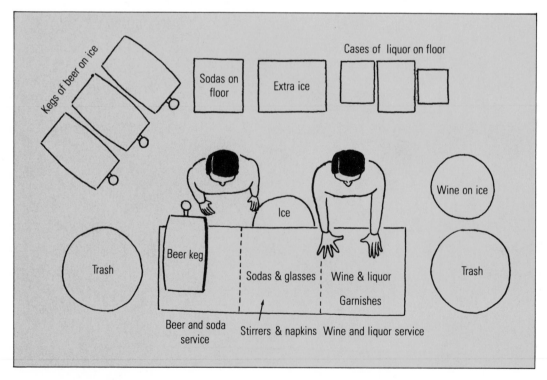

One-table service bar

Add the following for shaker cocktails:

1 long-handled spoon (iced tea spoon)
10-inch mixing glass
cocktail shaker

"A pro knows his pour" is the way professionals describe how a bartender consistently pours exactly the right amount of liquor. It takes a lot of practice to develop a "pour," but the volunteer can use the training tricks the pros begin with.

Felito starts novice bartenders out by having them use the distance between the end of their thumb and the first thumb knuckle as the pour measurement. This measurement produces a rather consistent 1½- to 2-ounce drink.

Steve recommends buying only liquor bottles with plastic pourers on top. "Set up the empty glass, tip the bottle about 45 to 60 degrees, and silently count two seconds of pouring per shot. This results in a consistent bar drink until you get enough experience to do it naturally."

"Pour into an empty glass, then fill the glass to the top with ice," says Felito. "Add the mix and the garnish, if any. Be as consistent as possible in your proportions. Remember, though, that a good bartender can 'read' people and won't get people drunk. He begins pouring lighter drinks if he sees a guest getting drunk, especially at the end of a party when people have to drive home."

Novice bartenders often need instructions in dealing with a bar full of eager customers. Felito tells new bartenders, "It's important to serve one customer at a time. Don't get ahead of yourself or you'll panic. You have to make it clear to the crowd right from the beginning.

"Stand in front of a customer and look him in the eye. Put a cocktail napkin down in front of him—that gesture tells the world you are serving him—and then say, 'What can I get you?' Be polite when other people try to muscle in. Tell them calmly, 'Excuse me, I'll be right with you,' and then turn back to the customer you are dealing with and fill his entire order.

"When you're filling a complicated order, set up the easy drinks first. The customer sees his order partially filled immediately and will let you alone. If, for example, your customer asks for two beers, two white wines, one red wine, one gin and tonic, one screwdriver, and a shot of tequila, you'd fill it as follows: First, get the red wine, white wines, shot of tequila, and the beers; then set out two glasses and pour gin in one and vodka in the other; fill with ice, tonic or juice, garnish, and sipstirs. Give it all to the customer to ferry back to his friends."

Consistency of drinks—in terms of proportion of alcohol to mixers regardless of who is bartending—is important, so go over the drink menu with the volunteers before the party, and then make a copy or two of it along with your "approved" recipes for cocktails. Put the recipes on a clipboard and hang it in the back of the bar space in case anybody needs to refer to it. Remember, the bartenders must *never* leave the bar untended.

Speed and efficiency are imperative to good beverage service. If people have to wait too long to get their drinks, the fun of the party is reduced, no matter how much time and money have been spent creating the perfect event.

Have the bar ready to go at least a half hour before the guests begin trickling in. If they have to go through a receiving line

BEVERAGE SERVICE

137

to get into the party space, your life will be easier. At some point, however, the room will be full and the bar will be crowded with guests who want to get back to their friends as fast as they can.

A professional bartender arrives at a party about two hours before it officially starts. He begins by checking tools and supplies to see if everything that was ordered is actually on site. Then he packs wine and beer in bags of ice and fills the Styrofoam coolers with ice.

His bar setup routine seldom varies and is usually done in this order:

1) Clean table and set out napkins, sipstirs, ashtrays, and matches;

2) Cut up all fruit; arrange garnishes within easy reach;

3) Make up any mixes, that is, Bloody Mary, and so forth;

4) Tap the beer keg;

5) Set out glasses;

6) Open bottles and get champagne ready;

7) Pour a few glasses of red wine;

8) When the party time is at hand, pour lots of glasses of white wine.

It's important that a bartender drink nothing alcoholic while working. Speed and efficiency count, and alcohol slows people down. Also, tending bar for a big crowd is very hard work. You're on your feet, hurrying to fill orders from beginning to end. Make sure your volunteers understand this and really want to do it.

▲▲▲▲▲▲▲▲

IF YOU DECIDE TO HIRE A PRO

▼▼▼▼▼▼▼

You may decide to hire a professional bartender to work the reception rather than recruit volunteers. Prices for bartenders vary in different parts of the country. On the East and West coasts, a professional expects to be paid between $85 and $110 for a five-hour party, plus his two-hour pre-party setup time. Guests do not tip at a private party, and no "tip cup" should be permitted on the bar. If the host and hostess are pleased with the service, they should tip him an extra $20 to $25 at the end of the event.

Try to locate a bartender through friends or ask at your favorite bar or restaurant. You need to be assured of his or her performance. If you have to resort to newspaper ads, be sure to get several references and check them all.

Once you find and hire the person you want, outline the drink menu and establish the dress code. Bartenders supply their own uniforms, so if you want a white shirt and black bow tie, or whatever, tell the bartender well in advance or the person may arrive wearing more casual clothes.

Another major point to discuss is overtime. If the party is marvelous, people often want it to continue even after the bride and groom have left. Alert your bartender to that possibility, if there is one, and work out an appropriate hourly pay for overtime.

The cleanup on the bar is done by the bartender, whether a pro or a friendly volunteer. Everything should be packed up to be returned for deposit, picked up by the rental company, taken back to somebody's house, or set out with the trash. This detail is especially important if you are in a rental space, so go over it in advance and avoid nasty surprises.

When Felito and Steve were asked to summarize their words of wisdom for novice bartenders, they said:

1) Plan everything carefully in advance;

2) Do as much of the work as possible before guests arrive;

3) Never leave the bar untended;

4) Always overbuy on the ice.

▼ *The Beverage Service worksheet can be found on pages 216–17.*

B E V E R A G E   S E R V I C E

▲▲▲▲▲▲▲

PHOTOGRAPHY

▼▼▼▼▼▼▼

13

PHOTOGRAPHY

Years from now you could be glowing over the memories your wedding photographs evoke, or you could be kicking yourself around the block for not having made sure your wedding pictures were terrific. It's a ▼ ▼ ▼ ▼ ▼ ▼ ▼ ▼ ▼ one-time event; either you get it or you don't. And you'll have the rest of your lives to ponder your photography decision!

The need for good photographs can arise months before the wedding, when you are planning your engagement party. Part of announcing the engagement is to send all the details to your local newspaper, along with a large black-and-white glossy photograph of the bride-to-be.

▲▲▲▲▲▲▲

NEWSPAPER ANNOUNCEMENTS AND PHOTOGRAPHY

▼▼▼▼▼▼▼

Newspapers want to print engagement and wedding announcements and photographs, but also they want to receive the information in a form that is most usable to them. The less work the society editor has to do to transform your good news into wording the paper can use, the better. Your life will be simpler, too, if you use the accepted wordings—you have only to fill in the blanks!

Plan to send the engagement and wedding press releases to all the papers in both the bride's and groom's hometowns, plus papers wherever you are currently residing. The written releases you send will be identical, and all newspapers should have the same date for release so your news will "hit the streets" on the same day. The photos, however, should not be identical. Newspapers in any one area are actually competing with one another and are happier when the visuals you send give each paper its own version of your story.

Several weeks prior to your engagement party telephone each newspaper in which you would like your announcement to appear. Ask to speak to somebody who handles weddings and engagements, probably the society editor or the home, family, or women's page editor. Tell that person you are planning to send the newspaper your engagement announcement and photograph, and you need to know how much in advance of the engagement party you should mail them the information.

Some papers will send you a form to fill in, thus assuring them that the data comes in easily usable form. Your phone call will get you that form with complete instructions as to timing, and so forth. If not, you'll be told when the paper would like to receive your release, generally about a week before you want it to appear.

The engagement and wedding press releases for the newspapers are somewhat standard. Traditionally, the parents of the bride make the engagement announcement, giving full mention to the parents of the groom in the very beginning. (Perhaps this is a throwback to days of arranged marriages?) The release goes on to announce the event and gives some identification for everybody mentioned. There's no point in trying to be creative; just send the facts in the accepted order, and they'll get published.

The press releases are always typed, double-spaced, on business-size paper. Do not use cute stationary or little informal note paper. Start with plain paper and head it with:

[Today's Date]
To: The Society Editor (Use name if possible)
For: Engagement Announcement
Release Date: Sunday, March 6, 1988

The body copy of your release will look something like this:

Mr. and Mrs. Joseph R. Jones of Wild Elk, Wyoming, announce the engagement of their daughter, Rosebud Marie, to Thomas Jefferson Smith, son of Mr. and Mrs. Andrew Carlyle Smith of Portland, Maine, and Key Largo, Florida.

PHOTOGRAPHY

Miss Jones, a graduate of the University of Oregon, is the Director of Research at the General Grass Corporation in Cleveland, Ohio. Mr. Smith graduated magna cum laude from the University of Pennsylvania, where he was elected to Phi Beta Kappa. He is a test pilot for Spaceshot Aviation, Little Falls, Idaho.

The wedding will take place in August, 1988.

That's basically it, with a few alternate wordings. If it's the second or third marriage for one or both people, for example, add an explanatory sentence on the end: "Mr. Smith's previous marriage ended in divorce" or "Miss Jones's previous marriages ended in divorce." If any of the parents have died, the parent identification should simply be, "Mrs. Rosalie J. Jones of Wild Elk, Wyoming, announces. . . ." If parents are divorced and/or remarried, give accurate identifications: "Mr. Joseph R. Jones of Port Said, California, and Mrs. Rosalie Jones Flugelhorn of Wild Elk, Wyoming, announce. . . ."

At the bottom of the press release type in the data the editor would need to get in touch with whoever announces the event. Remember, the bridal couple never announces the engagement if there is any relative, foster or blood kin, left on earth to do it for them! At the bottom of our mythical engagement press release there might be:

For further information contact:
Mrs. Joseph R. Jones
333 Park Crescent
Wild Elk, Wyoming 12345
(777) 123-4567

That's enough about the Smith/Jones nuptials. Now use the workbook page 202 to compose the wording for your own announcement.

A photograph of the bride, a head shot only, may accompany the announcement. Again, the newspapers need to have the picture in a usable form. Most American papers request either an 8-inch by 10-inch or 5-inch by 7-inch, black-and-white, glossy print. Do not send color photos or Polaroid shots. Since the bride will not be wearing wedding finery, any good black-and-white head shot, blown up to the correct size, can be sent. School yearbook photos often work very well, or any attractive candid shot that is sharp enough to reproduce clearly.

If you choose to send a photograph, you need to include a caption, identifying it and relating it to the press release. Professional publicists use the caption sheet not only for identification but also to protect the surface of the photograph so it will reproduce clearly.

Take a sheet of typing paper and type your identification, double-spaced, in the center of the page:

Miss Rosebud Marie Jones, whose engagement to Mr. Thomas Jefferson Smith is announced.

Then take the page and place it, with the typing on the inside, over the surface of the photo. Tape it to the lower back edge of the picture so that it opens down from the top and the identification can be read easily. Never write on the back or the front of a photograph!

Put the press release, the captioned photograph, and a sturdy piece of cardboard into a preaddressed manila envelope and mail it off, allowing enough time for the release to get to the paper by the desired date. (Never address the envelope after the photo is put inside; even the pressure of a pen on the outer envelope is enough to damage the surface of the photograph.)

The wedding announcement press release is more detailed than the engagement announcement. Years ago wedding write-ups were wildly detailed, with descriptions of everybody's clothes, the complete menu, and any celebrities on the guest list. Today much less information is included but enough so the reader gets an idea of the families involved.

This time the photograph will be of the bride or both the bride and groom in their wedding outfits. If the bridal portrait isn't available, don't send another copy of the head shot that accompanied the engagement announcement. Editors get very upset if they find they've inadvertently repeated themselves; nothing is deader than yesterday's news.

The release, typed double-spaced, is headed up the same way as the engagement release:

[Today's Date]
To: The Society Editor (use the name)
For: Wedding Announcement
Release Date: Sunday, August 14, 1988

The release date is important since the bride's married name is used, and she doesn't have the legal use of the name until after the ceremony. The release should appear in the newspapers the day after the wedding if at all possible. If you are getting married on a Wednesday, have your release dated for the Thursday edition. If the paper is a weekly, aim for the first issue following the ceremony.

The wedding announcement press release will read:

Rosebud Marie Jones, daughter of Mr. and Mrs. Joseph R. Jones of Wild Elk, Wyoming, was married yesterday to Thomas Jefferson Smith, son of Mr. and Mrs. Andrew Carlyle Smith of Portland, Maine, and Key Largo, Florida. The Reverend Michael Brown performed the ceremony at the Second Presbyterian Church of Wild Elk.

Dahlia Elaine Jones was maid of honor for her sister. The groom's uncle, Rear Admiral Louis Campbell Brown, was the best man.

Mrs. Smith, a graduate of the University of Oregon, is the Director of Research of General Grass Corporation, Cleveland, Ohio. Her father is founder and president of the Elk Hoof Shoe Company in Cheyenne. Her mother, Rosalie Jones, is Director of the Save the Coyote Foundation in Wild Elk. Her paternal grandfather served in the Wyoming State Legislature from 1916 to 1924.

Mr. Smith graduated magna cum laude from the University of Pennsylvania where he was elected to Phi Beta Kappa. He is a test pilot for Spaceshot Aviation in Little Falls, Idaho. His father is the owner of the *Portland Daily Bugle*, in Portland, Maine, and an adjunct professor of journalism at the Free Enterprise College in Portland. His mother, Lolita Smith, is a public health nurse. The groom is the grandson of the late Edgar F. Smith, inventor of the Smith cranberry harvester.

PHOTOGRAPHY

For further information contact:
Mrs. Joseph R. Jones
333 Park Crescent
Wild Elk, Wyoming 12345
(777) 123-4567

The same rules apply for wedding announcements as for engagements if parents are divorced and remarried, and so forth.

The photograph that accompanies the wedding announcement should be captioned:

Mrs. Thomas Jefferson Smith, whose marriage took place yesterday.

or:

Mr. and Mrs. Thomas Jefferson Smith, whose wedding took place yesterday.

Use the same careful procedure for captioning and mailing the announcement and photo. Again, use a piece of cardboard and address the envelope before you insert the photograph.

Use the workbook page 203 to write out your wedding announcement.

▲▲▲▲▲▲▲

PHOTOGRAPHING THE CEREMONY

▼▼▼▼▼▼▼

The success a volunteer photographer will have covering your wedding depends, to a certain extent, on the camera he or she uses. New York photographer Erica Evans, whose wedding photos are cherished by many metropolitan area couples, strongly recommends that you rent the appropriate equipment if your volunteer's gear is less than state-of-the-art.

"Speed is the critical element," says Erica, "so borrow or rent a 35-millimeter fully automatic camera with a flash arm and a gel cell to power the batteries. And get it enough in advance so you can play with it and be comfortable shooting, even if it means two rentals, one the weekend before and one on the weekend of the wedding. There are no retakes at a wedding."

Erica's camera description needs some explanations. The 35 millimeter fully automatic camera should be fitted with an extension called a flash arm. This screws onto the camera and moves the flashbulb off to the side of the camera. The flash arm guarantees no "red eye effect," that dreadful occurrence when the subject is hit directly in the eyes with the flash. If you've seen animals looking directly into the headlights of a car, that's red eye.

The gel cell hooks into the flash and replaces the AA batteries you usually use. It works instantly, so you don't have to wait for your flash to recycle before shooting a second picture. One gel cell is good for about four hundred shots, which is about what you'll need.

"Never shoot a wedding without using a gel cell," warns Erica. "You'll miss too much. You need to use a flash for every shot, no matter what the ambient light is. With a regular camera you'd be able to get only one shot of the couple coming down the aisle. You need to shoot as many as you can—one shot might not tell the story!"

Erica recommends bringing fifteen rolls of thirty-six-exposure color print film to a wedding (not slide film). She shoots between ten and eleven rolls for an average wedding but has the extra film for backup. She estimates each roll of film will cost about twenty dollars, including processing, so her basic budgeting, exclusive of her fee, begins at around three hundred dollars per wedding. Since the film will be color, it cannot be processed successfully at home.

THE BRIDAL PORTRAIT

Photographing the bridal portrait can be done as soon as the wedding clothes and accessories are available. The more lead time, the better, since the tension grows as the big day approaches. Everyone concerned wants the bride to look as serene and carefree as possible!

Erica begins her wedding coverage by meeting with the bride and groom and asking what sort of photos they really like. She asks to see examples of any pictures they adore and shows some of her work to establish the ground rules. Once Erica and the couple are clear on the point of view, she is ready to proceed.

"The more formal the portrait, the easier it is for the photographer," says Erica. "There is less interpretation in a head shot than there is in something with more action and expression, so it's a good place to begin.

"I go to the bride's home, preferably in the morning when the sun is quite strong, and we select a location for the portrait. Avoid plain white walls! I opt for a nice

Fill card

PHOTOGRAPHY

window that has lots of light pouring in, and we arrange her, in her outfit, in front of the window.

"The sunlight is the primary source of light. I also want a secondary source to fill out the shadows on the unlighted side of her face, so I use what the professionals call a 'fill card' that reflects light onto the shadow side. A fill card can be made from a piece of bright white cardboard the size of a sheet of typing paper. Get somebody to hold the fill card so that the reflected light softens the dark shadows. Move the card around until you get the effect you want.

"Shoot a number of pictures, as described above, to be sent out to the newspapers with the press releases. Then put a diffusion filter on your camera and shoot an equal number in soft focus as part of the wedding picture collection. The newspapers need a very sharp photograph to reproduce well, but the couple wants soft, lovely pictures to keep forever."

Andrew K. Marcus, of New York's Fred Marcus Photographers, offers other diffusion techniques. "Stretch a piece of a black nylon stocking tightly over the lens and shoot through it. The black stocking softens and diffuses. Don't use a white stocking because it will cause a glare. If you want to make a soft focus filter, coat the edges of a filter with clear nail polish or petroleum jelly. Both will soften and diffuse."

Andy Marcus says he meets the bride's family well in advance to plan the wedding. The planning is crucial since the photographer must be at the right place at the right time. He asks the bride's family to indicate who is directing or stage managing the event so that the photographer will have a contact point who can cue him to the activities.

At a Marcus Photographers' wedding, formal portraits of the bridal party are taken about an hour before the wedding. Everybody is dressed and ready, and posing the group shots is easier, Andy feels, before anything else happens to distract the party.

In addition to the formal group portraits, a Marcus photographer will take many preplanned "human interest" photos before the ceremony. "We try to catch the warmth of the day, the feeling among members of the wedding. We photograph the bride and groom, bride and her mother, bride and her father, bride and brother, groom and mother, and so forth, covering all the possible combinations. Then we photograph the bride and mother getting ready, walking to the car, the attendants outside the church, and so on. We show all the dresses full-length and try to get the front and back of the wedding gown. We might shoot one hundred pictures before the couple leaves for the church."

Erica Evans has a slightly different approach. She takes the formal group portraits at the beginning of the reception and concentrates on the candids beforehand. "People are much too tense to get good formal photographs right before the ceremony. I shoot lots of candids and try to get action and motion as well as emotion in them. By the time the wedding day arrives I've gotten to know the bride and her family, so it's easier."

PHOTOGRAPHING THE CEREMONY

Many churches, temples, and synagogues have rules against photographs being taken during the ceremony. Refer to your Ceremony Checklist, page 194, and remember to ask your ushers to tell guests who come, camera in hand, to abide by the rules. If photographs are allowed during the ceremony, be wary of overshooting. Many amateurs get carried away and overshoot at the church, leaving them short of film for the reception. There are only a few photo opportunities during the ceremony: processional, father giving bride to groom, exchange of rings, the kiss, and recessional.

The beginning of the reception is an important time for the photographer. If your volunteer photographer knows just about everybody on the guest list, he or she can work alone. If not, assign somebody who does know most of the guests to work with the photographer to make sure nobody is missed. A good spot to place the photographer is just inside the door of the reception space. Get a photo or two of every person or couple as they come in. They'll be looking happy, well groomed, and will be too much in a hurry to freeze up when they notice the camera pointing at them.

Give your volunteer plenty of help, making sure he or she is at hand before any of the traditional parts of the reception take place. A copy of Ken Deutsch's description of the Fairmont wedding protocol in Chapter 4 will be helpful, giving the volunteer some idea of the sequence of events.

After the wedding, when the prints and negatives come back from being processed, one final bit of work remains. Before you show anything to anybody, sit down with a nonsmear pen and label the prints so they match the negatives. Each roll of film will have a letter on it; each frame on each negative strip will have a number underneath it. Match each print with its negative and write the roll letter and frame number in ink on the bottom of every print. It's the only way to keep everything straight and avoid having to look through all four hundred prints each time you want to order a print!

▲▲▲▲▲▲▲

VIDEOTAPE

▼▼▼▼▼▼▼

Videotaping has become a popular way to record a wedding, and the increase in Beta and VHS equipment sales promises to make videotaping a standard wedding activity in the near future. Most people do not yet own a video camera, but they are rented easily in most parts of the country.

My son, Mills R. Clark, a video director of photography, says, "Ask for a portable, battery-operated, ½-inch consumer color video camera and recorder. Many of these have the tape deck with a condenser mike built right onto the back of the camera so you don't need cables, mikes, or other gear. The camera will weigh about 10 or 12 pounds, including the tape.

"The camera will use VHS or Beta tape, the kind that costs between five and seven dollars at record and tape stores.

P H O T O G R A P H Y

PHOTOGRAPHY

You can tape up to two hours on a piece of tape, so get an extra cassette or two for the wedding and reception. Ask the rental person about the life span of the batteries and get enough extra batteries, plus a backup, to cover the time. Remember, there are no retakes at a wedding."

Mills recommends renting the equipment a day or so in advance. "Make sure you get the owner's manual with the rental and ask the rental person to show you all the features. Tell the rental person what you're doing and that you need equipment sensitive enough to use with "available light." That's the key phrase; if there's any doubt about the equipment, keep on shopping.

"Play with the equipment, shooting on an old cassette, until you feel comfortable with it. You can't get creative until you are at ease with the camera. Concentrate on the steadiness of the camera. Practice making all of your movements (walking, panning, carrying) smooth and fluid. When you're rolling tape, think of the camera as a set of eyes you're holding. Don't shake them up; treat those eyes delicately.

"Also, don't always have the camera on your shoulder. Shoot from the hip, rest the camera on a table, cradle it in your arms. The more flexible you are, the more interesting your tape will be."

Advance planning is perhaps even more critical in videotaping than it is in still photography. You will need to appoint somebody to identify guests to the camera person, and make sure nobody is left out. Supply a written schedule of events to your video volunteer early on so a story

line can be established. The videotape will be a documentary of your wedding and will benefit from using documentary film techniques.

Develop a point of view. The camera can tell the story from the point of view of the bride, the groom, an interested observer, or anybody you choose. Select your point of view and stick with it, taping only what that person could really observe. Don't mix points of view or your tape will lack clarity and impact.

Mills says, "Think about the viewer and how you can make the story come alive for him. The camera will do long shots, wide shots, zooms, and close-up reaction shots. You'll probably want to start with lots of wide shots so the viewer can get the feel of the place and then begin building your story by playing off wide shots and close-ups. You've got to tell a story slowly enough so the viewer can follow it. Amateurs generally shoot too fast and whiz the camera around. Professionals shoot slowly, lingering on shots. You can pause the camera on some action and then zoom in and get close-up reaction shots from the people standing near you.

"Fun additions to put into your documentary are on-the-spot interviews with guests. Whenever there's a lull in the action, go over to guests and tape their comments. Usually they're very funny and loving, and they punctuate the momentous quality of the occasion.

"Professionals always go on a pre-shoot survey. Before I shoot a wedding I go on a survey to scope out the rooms, see the lighting, check the bride's and groom's sides. I look for any raised area or access to a balcony, anything that will give me extra flexibility and make the tape more interesting. If I'm taping the ceremony, I want to know if they'll be kneeling or standing, and when, so I can plan what I'm going to do in advance."

Work with your video volunteer to establish a story line and operating procedure. Use the workbook pages 218–19, photocopying the final copy for the video on-site checklist. That way, nobody has to try to remember everything, and none of the crucial parts of the celebration will be missed.

Both the still photographer and the video camera person need to be uninvolved in partying. Unless they tend to business from beginning to end they're not going to come up with really good documentation. Unless your volunteers are willing to forgo some of the carefree fun, you might be better off hiring outsiders. If you decide to do this, be sure to check references and see several samples of completely finished work. Finally, make up a letter of agreement, following the sample in Chapter 9, Sound, and get a signed copy for your files.

▼ *The Announcement worksheets can be found on pages 202–3. The Photography worksheet can be found on pages 218–19.*

P H O T O G R A P H Y

▲▲▲▲▲▲▲

14

PLANNING THE WEDDING FEAST: ADVANCE WORK, INCLUDING THE CAKE

▼▼▼▼▼▼▼

The difference between a bunch of friends getting together and doing potluck and a bunch of friends getting together and doing a major food presentation is simply the planning," says Diane McIngvale, owner, with Mike Hearn, of Dallas's famous Chow Catering.

Take Diane's word for it. Whether you've decided to prepare the food for a small wedding dinner or for a large reception, you have to do a great deal of planning and organizing. Your wedding is a very special, once-in-a-lifetime event, and you don't want the food to look like just another party.

The first decision to make is often the easiest—whether to have a buffet or a sit-down meal. If your guest list runs much over thirty people, sit-down service is unworkable. Hotels and restaurants can do it; loving volunteers cannot.

The time of day may influence your choices. A luncheon buffet need not be as substantial as one presented at dinnertime. A midafternoon reception might offer only hors d'oeuvres followed by the wedding cake. A late evening buffet could duplicate the luncheon menu. On the other hand, you may decide to put together a wonderful feast of favorite foods you and your guests will enjoy regardless of the hour.

There are no hard-and-fast rules other than having some kind of wedding cake to share with guests. Actually, in the wilder days of the 1960s I once attended a wedding where cupcakes were substituted for a cake, and it was pretty terrible. So do plan to have a wedding cake and surround it with whatever pleases you both.

The presentation and the service are what make fantastic party food different from ordinary food. You and your volunteers can produce delicious food, right? But when it's presented on a garnished platter in combination with other decorated treats and served from a beautifully appointed, artfully lighted buffet table, it becomes memorable party food.

▲▲▲▲▲▲▲▲

HOW TO ORGANIZE YOUR BUFFET SERVICE

▼▼▼▼▼▼▼

Before you begin menu planning, give some thought to the service that will make the party special. Diane advises that "when you sit down to plan a major party, know very clearly what you want. If your friends are going to help you, be strong enough to guide them. Catering is hard work. You need to set up an organizational structure before you even begin to talk about what to serve."

Diane continues, "Let's start with the four crucial areas in catering. The kitchen is first, the buffet is next, and the bar is the third. The last, more an activity than an area, is busing, the professional term for cleanup.

"To make a large party run smoothly you need a person in charge of each area. These area managers work together to keep the traffic flowing, because if any one area slows down, the whole party will be headed for disaster. A professional caterer would have the four managers coordinated by a food manager who is responsible to the overall party planner. A chain of command exists. And it really works."

This might seem like more organization than you and your friends would be comfortable with. It's difficult enough to tell friends what to do, especially when they are trying to be as helpful as can be! If your reception is going to be really large, however, you would be wise to incorporate some of Diane's chain of command.

By recruiting a food manager you make sure neither of you nor your parents will end up running around the reception worrying about the food. The food manager you are looking for is a whiz at administration. The best person for this job may not even know how to boil water. Pick somebody who will remain cool under fire.

"At some moment all brides become hysterical," Diane explains. "The most down-to-earth, sophisticated, mature women become basket cases at one point or another. You need someone there to say, 'Calm down, it'll be all right.'"

If possible, have your food manager help you recruit the four area managers so the chain of command is clear from the very beginning. Refer to the chapter on beverage service for job descriptions of your bartenders and the bar boy. Appoint one person to head up each bar shift. Here's how the four areas work together:

The *kitchen manager* is in charge of the kitchen but may not have much to do with the actual cooking of anything. He or she supervises kitchen workers, making sure the food looks marvelous and arrives promptly at the buffet table or gets passed for hors d'oeuvres. No plate or platter leaves the kitchen without the manager's okay. The kitchen manager is the "inside" person.

The *buffet manager* is the "outside" person, stationed near the buffet. He or she supervises people who actually carve or serve the food. The buffet manager also is responsible for keeping the buffet functioning and attractive looking. The buffet manager and the kitchen manager work together, speeding up or slowing down the pace of the food service to make the party flow smoothly.

The *busing manager* has nothing at all to do with the food but can make or break a party. Of all the jobs involved in putting on any big party, busing or cleanup is the one most often overlooked by nonfood professionals. And it's crucial! Your busing manager will supervise several volunteers, since no one person can take care of any sizable party. The busing people move discreetly around the party space during the celebration, cleaning up and removing debris before it can accumulate. A well hidden trash area needs to be delineated beforehand so the manager has a place to stack filled garbage bags. If the busing is done properly, there is no huge mess to clean up after the party.

The number of workers you'll need depends a great deal on what you plan to serve. "For a one-hundred-person party catered by Chow," Diane said, "there would be two people in the kitchen, one on the buffet if nothing needed to be carved or served out, three people busing, and perhaps one to pass hors d'oeuvres just to keep things flowing. The bar service, of course, would be extra."

▲▲▲▲▲▲▲

CHOOSING PARTY FOOD WISELY AND WELL

▼▼▼▼▼▼▼

Take your time designing the menu for the reception. There are entirely too many choices to consider, recipes to try, and prices to check. Think about the foods you and your friends adore; remember wonderful feasts your family has shared. Add to those the seasonal foods that will be at their peak around the time of your wedding. Certain foods signify certain activities: hot dogs at a ball game, cotton candy at the circus. What foods say "lovely party" to you?

Also think about your budget. You have X amount of dollars to serve food to X amount of guests. Caterers usually charge by the head. You might pay eight to twelve dollars per person for a modest cocktail/hors d'oeuvres reception. A buffet might be twenty-two to thirty dollars and a sit-down meal from thirty-five dollars on up. These price estimates aren't going to save you money, but they certainly help put the food money into perspective.

European-trained Jane Keller, owner/

cook of the Country Kitchen in Phoenicia, New York, suggests focusing on eye appeal when you plan any party menu. "Think of an empty plate, then imagine people filling up that plate so it all looks tantalizingly appetizing. You certainly want a variety of colors, sizes, and textures on the plate. How awful if everything is pale, creamy and mayonnaised, or if it all looks limp and mushy! Treat your imaginary plate as if it were a canvas and you are painting the best looking party plate you can conjure up."

Jane recommends keeping it simple: "Choose no more than four or five major dishes for a buffet. A typical menu would include one meat, a fish or poultry dish, a carbohydrate dish such as a pasta salad, a marinated tomato and mozzarella platter, and a vegetable combination, plus a dessert. I skip green salads; nobody eats them at weddings. And remember, the presentation is what is important."

Diane McIngvale takes it a bit further: "When I talk to a client with a limited budget I often suggest just fruit and cheese, plus crudités and dip. The client will say that's not enough, so I say, 'Let's talk about the display of these items.' That's a very full picture. There's no need to have seven different items. Just strawberries and Brie can be a beautiful display." Diane whipped out a photo of a Chow Catering buffet consisting of an incredible tower of strawberries cascading around creamy rounds of Brie. Her point was well taken.

To Henry Archer Meer, the *chef de garde manger* at Lutece, New York's internationally famous restaurant, the menu planning starts with the decision concerning whether to serve hot or cold foods or a combination of both. The no-kitchen party space can limit you somewhat, unless you are willing to set up field stoves and/or rent warming ovens.

Henry suggests balancing the entire menu, even the hors d'oeuvres, to include the major food categories: meat, fish and seafood, poultry, cheese, grains and breads, vegetables, fruits, and sweets.

"Try not to repeat a category. If shrimp are part of the hors d'oeuvres, for example, don't include them in a seafood Newburg. A collection of great cheeses surrounded by baskets of interesting breads is a natural for the hors d'oeuvre table, but then don't serve a cheese dish in the buffet.

"See if you can make the buffet a bit dramatic," he advises. "Think about building a buffet around the carving of several room temperature meats or a selection of meat, fish, and poultry. Make one buffet table the carving board and have three people behind the table, ready to carve from a large meat roast, a whole poached fish, and a big roasted turkey. Surround these with a variety of piping hot and well chilled pouring sauces. Use small fondue burners to heat the hot sauces, and present the cold sauce bowls over beds of ice. Americans are meat oriented, and they love carving boards, plus you'll add the drama of sauces bubbling over flames. Best of all, this is a service nonprofessionals can do very well."

Jane Keller's legendary room temperature buffets are often built around selections of interesting sauces that guests can put on cooked meat, fish, and poultry. "I have a group of sauce bases I use over and over again, with different flavorings and spices:

157

Mayonnaise: Can be flavored to go in many directions, such as horseradish, curry, tomato, orange juice, and so forth. I make my own mayonnaise, so it won't contain the sugar the commercial ones do, and I add some water to thin it and make it silky.

Vinaigrette: Oil and vinegar, basically, but the great variety of oils and vinegars give it vast potential. Vinaigrette can be flavored with all kinds of herbs and spices.

Pesto: Fresh herbs are combined with ground nuts, oils, and spices; unusual and appetizing.

Fruit: Dried, fresh, or canned fruits are stewed in the juices from roasted meats or in consomme and then reduced to a flavorful gloss.

Gravy or meat juices: The basic brown sauce has variations such as bordelaise."

You may decide to combine carving with hot food service. Have one roast or a baked ham to carve, for example, plus a few sauces, and then add curried chicken or other casserole dishes. Since you know the food preferences of many of your guests, select the dishes you know will be a hit.

Alan S. Munn, the food manager on one of Chandris Fantasy Cruises' ships, the *S.S. Amerikanis,* is a master at buffet planning. Cruise ships are famous for their fabulous buffets, and Alan's *S.S. Amerikanis* presentations are knockouts! He tells us, "Think variety. That's what counts. People want to walk into a buffet and be overwhelmed by good things. We hear this a lot on the ship because we have a captive audience. They see everything we put out, day after day. It has to look exciting each and every time.

"People are funny when it comes to food. They really want variety. If you have a wonderful feast, built around incredible baked hams, many people will come away saying, 'It was nice, but all they served was ham. . . .' It's best to plan smaller amounts of many, many items.

"The buffet is the most inexpensive way to serve a large crowd. There's a psychological element in a buffet service when you have a lot of people going through the line. My company has developed figures on this: Chandris figures one out of twenty-five or twenty-six people actually fill up their plates. Other than that one, it's a little slice of this, a little piece of that. People don't want to appear gluttonous.

"Many catering books suggest planning ¼ to ½ pound of meat per person at a buffet. We feel that's nonsense. There's no way anyone will take 4 ounces or more in a buffet line. They would have to stand there, taking slice after slice; it just doesn't happen. And if you want to control the food consumption even more, use servers to place the food on the guests' plates. We know that only one out of every thirty people will say, 'May I please have another slice?'

"Everything stems from the setup of the buffet. This is basic professional food service information, and you'll spot it whenever you attend a professional buffet. To begin with, you always set up the inexpensive, bulky items first. That includes pasta dishes, potato and macaroni salads, green salads, and the breads and rolls. Next comes the medium expensive items such as cheeses, deviled eggs, and your vegetable dishes. Put the expensive meats, fish, and poultry last and surround them with a variety of garnishes.

PLANNING THE WEDDING FEAST

"People usually like potato salad and pasta, so they take some. By the time they reach the expensive items they've already filled up their plates and have only about one-fourth of the plate left for meat. Keep this in mind when you do your menu planning. Pick a budget figure, but then see if it's really realistic to try to feed your number of guests. At three dollars a head your menu will have to be different from four dollars a head. After you get the money figured out, plan the best menu you can, put it away for a week or two, then go back and review it. See what changes you want to make before you begin trying out recipes."

Permit me to add one additional caveat: Make sure most, if not all, of the dishes you choose can be made the day before. Avoid omelets, hot soufflés, flambéed dishes. Anything that will require on-the-spot cooking should not be on your menu. If you are having a fruit salad, keep it down to five or six kinds of fruit, omitting bananas. Prepare the individual fruits, but do not combine them until the morning of the wedding. If you are dressing foods with mayonnaise, prepare the dish but do not add the chilled dressing until serving time. This is for safety more than convenience. Mayonnaise decays rapidly at room temperature, and you certainly don't want to poison your guests!

The wedding reception kitchen should not be a "cooking kitchen." Transport the foods to the party space in their most readied state. Use the hours before the reception to dress the food, arrange the platters, decorate with garnishes made the day before, warm the foods that need to be served hot, and arrange the buffet tables according to the design you had planned in advance.

Figuring out how much you need for a large party is always difficult. Different people have different appetites, and each person's appetite varies from day to day. Accept the fact that there will always be some waste; the trick is to try to keep that waste to a minimum. As Jane cheerfully points out, "People never eat as much as you fear they will." Here are some guidelines from the professionals:

Hors d'oeuvres: Four per person per hour. Pick out about six kinds of canapes and duplicate them in sufficient quantity for everybody.

Crudités: 2 ounces per person if other canapes are being served; 3½ ounces if you're serving only crudités, dip, and fruit and cheese.

Meat, poultry, and fish: 3 ounces per person. Increase this a bit if you are offering a carving board. Almost everybody will want a taste of each dish. Usually roast beef is the most popular and fish the least, so order accordingly.

Fruit salad: 1 to 2 ounces per person.

Supplementary dishes (such as vegetable combinations, pasta, salads, and so forth): 1½ ounces per person per dish.

Breads: one to one and a half slices per person. All breads must be sliced in advance.

Dessert: 3 to 4 ounces per person.

Integrate these guidelines with your knowledge of your guests and your own common sense; for example, if you know everybody in your crowd is mad for sesame noodles, increase the estimated portion size a bit, perhaps to 3 ounces per person.

A non-wedding cake dessert should be served following the buffet, along with coffee and tea. The dessert can be light and rather simple. Plates of fancy cookies work well or cookies plus a fresh fruit bowl or a chilled mousse. Again, avoid anything that requires extra care, such as ice cream.

▲▲▲▲▲▲▲

THE WEDDING CAKE

▼▼▼▼▼▼▼

The wedding cake, or bride's cake, is traditionally a multitiered white cake with white icing that is fancifully decorated and topped with a nonedible decoration. Sometimes the top layer is a white fruitcake that is not served at the reception but taken home and frozen for a reappearance at the first anniversary celebration. Personally, I feel this is truly one of the myths surrounding a wedding. I've never come across anyone who has ever heard of the defrosted, year-old cake being a taste treat, much less even edible. Think twice about giving freezer space to this probable disaster.

The groom's cake, native to the southern and southwestern parts of the country, generally is a fudgy chocolate sheet cake decorated with chocolate icing and often containing fruits and/or liqueurs. In areas where the groom's cake is served, it is presented along with the bride's cake. The traditional cutting of the wedding cake is done on the bride's cake only. Guests are served a small slice of each cake on the same plate. Reports from Texas and the Southwest favor the luscious groom's cake over the bride's two to one!

Any cake recipe you like can be used for your wedding cake in lieu of the rather bland white-on-white baker's cake.

Choose chocolate or spice cake or carrot cake or layers of different kinds of cake. What makes the bride's cake a standout is the icing decorations and the tiering. The decoration for the top of the cake can be purchased at most party stores or bakeries that supply wedding cakes. A cascade of fresh flowers makes a charming decoration for the cake if you are not wild about the little bride and groom figures or the sparkly wedding bell.

The amount of cake to bake depends on the number of guests. Wedding cake must be served to everyone but is something guests never can have seconds on, so figure on one slice per person. Slices can be 1 inch wide, so measure around the outer rim of your cake pans and note how many 1-inch slices you will have per layer.

Gisella Heinemann, owner of Gisella's Secrets, an exciting New York City bakery, diagrams the cutting and, there-

Wedding cake decorated with fresh flowers

fore, the amount by making each slice 1 inch wide by 2 inches long as follows:

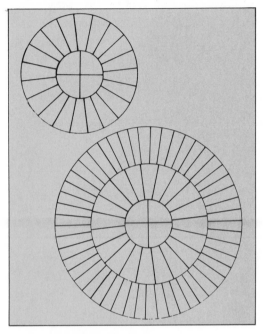

Cutting cake layers

Cake decorating equipment is sold in the gourmet section of department stores or kitchen shops. Complete directions come with the equipment plus recipes for the different kinds of icing recommended for leaves, initials, and so forth. Research cake decorations in bridal magazines and at local bakeries after you experiment with the equipment and become familiar with the shapes your equipment can produce. Sketch the designs you like and post them in front of you when you decorate.

Mastering the equipment so you can create great looking decorations takes some practice but is well within the grasp of any interested person. Also, you can work in increments. If you get the festoons down pat, for example, you can use

tiny live flowers and leaves tucked in wherever a blossom should occur. Nobody says the entire cake has to be edible.

Professional bakers arrange cakes in tiers because the sheer weight of many layers stacked on each other would be disastrous. The tiers may be separated, or they may appear to sit one on top of the other. The bottom tier is generally larger than the upper ones; the very top tier is often quite small. The layers can be round, square, rectangular, whatever shape you like. For unusually shaped layers, bake large sheet cakes, make a paper pattern, and cut out the shapes with a sharp knife.

Bakers tell us timing is important when doing a large party cake. Fresh cake is very difficult to work with, so allow your layers to sit, well wrapped in plastic, at least twenty-four hours before you ice and decorate them. Uniced layers can be frozen and then defrosted and decorated the day before the wedding. The professional bakeries that specialize in wedding cakes generally bake large quantities of their standard-size cake layers and then freeze them to use as cake orders come in.

As soon as you know how many layers you need to bake, you can begin planning the tiers. Each layer will need to sit on top of a rigid board. Thin plywood or very heavy cardboard cut to shape works just fine; cover the boards with foil or with heavy white butcher's paper stapled or taped to fit snugly.

For a cake with separated layers, collect enough identical empty cans (in a height higher than a layer) to separate the layers. Remove the tops and bottoms of the cans and cover each can with heavy white paper glued together with rubber cement.

When you're ready to do the cake, put each uniced layer onto a covered rigid base. Place a can (or two) in the bottom layer, pushing it down into the cake to make a hole. Remove and discard the center cake piece, leaving an opening. Set the can back in the opening, balance the next board and layer on top of it, and repeat the procedure until you have the uniced cake set up in tiers.

If you are happy with the balance, take it all apart and begin icing the individual layers. If you don't like the overall look,

change the size of the cans and keep adjusting until it looks good to you. Decorate according to your design and chill to set the icing. Some bakeries spread a thin film of icing on top of the paper around the cans so it will all look unified. If the plain cans look out of place, ice them when icing the cake so they have time to set.

Transport the decorated cake layers in individual boxes to the party space. Assemble the cake after the buffet service is over and the guests are partying. If fresh flowers are part of the cake, add them just before the presentation. It's wise to carry

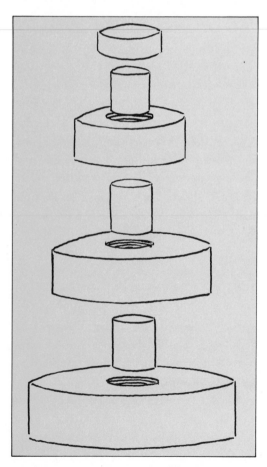

Cake tier assembly for separated layers

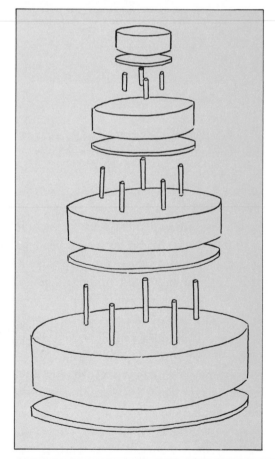

Cake tier assembly with wooden dowels for nonseparated layers

a pastry bag with some extra icing with you to the reception in case you have some fix-up work to do when you unbox the layers.

Gisella tells us the nonseparated layers are done in similar manner but without the cans. Place the uniced layers on the prepared heavy cardboard bases. Get a small supply of round, thin, wooden dowels or chopsticks and cut them to the height of each cake layer. To assemble the cake, push a circle of dowels down into the bottom layer to support the next layer, and so on, up to the top.

Gisella, known for her imaginatively decorated wedding and party cakes, gave us recipes and techniques she swears nonprofessionals can use to achieve great looking decorations. And she's right. We used them with great success, and so can you. Also, once you learn how to do some of the basic items you'll be the star of every fund-raising bazaar and cake sale for the rest of your days!

Gisella began by discussing children's modeling clay, the clay-dough stuff that's part of every kindergarten. Bakers use their own versions of clay-dough to create flowers, leaves, creatures, and anything else that can pretty up a cake. She gave us recipes for a marzipan modeling dough and a mock fondant for molding. They are virtually identical for use, except the marzipan will taste of almonds while the fondant can be flavored with anything you like. Choose whichever sounds good to you. Both are colored with vegetable food colors, available at supermarkets.

All measurements are approximate because of diverse factors such as humidity and the density of different brands. "Work toward getting a clay-dough consistency," she says. "Add tiny amounts of liquid or solid if it doesn't feel quite right. Remember, nothing is absolute. Get a consistency any child could play with, and you're ready to begin modeling."

MARZIPAN MODELING DOUGH

1 pound almond paste
¼ cup light (clear) corn syrup
1 cup confectioners' sugar

Almond paste is available in most supermarkets in the baking section. Buy the best grade you can since it will be the whitest and will look best when food coloring is added. "Odense" is a good nationally distributed brand.

Before combining the ingredients sieve together 1 cup of cornstarch with 1 cup of confectioners' sugar. You'll use this to "flour" the countertop or pastry board you'll work on and your hands, so the dough doesn't stick. Then crumble the almond paste into a bowl, add the syrup and unsieved confectioners' sugar, and work it into a dough. When most of it is together, sprinkle the cornstarch mixture onto your work space and turn the dough out onto it. Knead it until smooth, adding extra confectioners' sugar if necessary. Keep tightly covered until ready to use.

MOCK FONDANT FOR MOLDING

6 cups confectioners' sugar
1 large egg white (unbeaten)
3 tablespoons light corn syrup

You'll need to make the cornstarch and sugar combo here too, keeping a bowl of it handy to prevent the dough from sticking. Put the 6 cups of confectioners' sugar in a bowl. Warm the syrup until it is quite runny (not hot) and add it together with egg white all at once. Combine with your hands, then turn out onto the board sprinkled with the cornstarch mix. Knead until smooth. Wrap it tightly in plastic wrap and let rest for ten minutes or so. Fondant hardens more rapidly than the marzipan, so rewrap it immediately after working with it.

To color either of the doughs, pinch off some dough, make an indentation in the center of it, and sprinkle on a drop or two of vegetable food coloring. Knead it in your hands to distribute the color, adding more color if needed. Cover tightly until you are ready to use it.

Now for the flowers and leaves: After

molding them, let them dry in the air until hard. Store them, not touching, in airtight containers, such as Tupperware, and refrigerate or freeze. They will keep for at least a week in the refrigerator and for about a month in the freezer. To defrost for use, place in the refrigerator overnight.

Let's begin with a carnation. Use the vegetable food coloring liquid to color a walnut-sized piece of dough an appropriate carnation color. Using the cornstarch mix on a pastry board, roll out a strip about 5 inches long, tapering from 1 inch to about 1½ inches in width. With a small, sharp knife, make cuts every ¼ inch. Cut halfway down the strip, leaving

Making a carnation

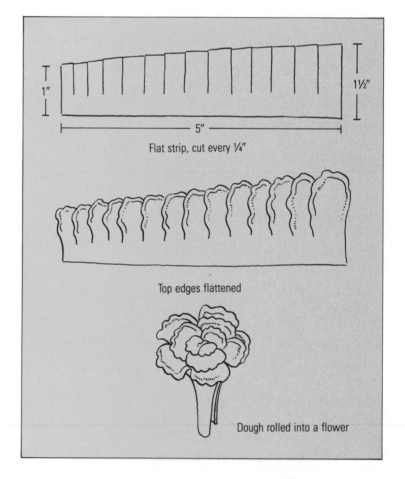

1"

1½"

5"

Flat strip, cut every ¼"

Top edges flattened

Dough rolled into a flower

the bottom edge uncut. With your finger-nail or the tip of a small table knife, press the top end of each cut piece, flattening it into a slightly jagged edge. With a pastry brush or a small paintbrush, remove all of the cornstarch. Begin rolling the strip, starting from the thin end. Pinch the bottom together and gently open up the petals and shape them to look flowerlike.

Next, let's make a rose. Use a walnut-sized piece of colored dough. Pinch off some to make a cone shape about 1 inch high, flattening the bottom so it will stand up. Nip off a little piece of dough, flatten it with your fingers, and place it, slightly folded, on the top of the cone to form the closed-up center of the rose. Use a touch of egg white to keep it on if the cone is very dry. Pinch off other small pieces and flatten them into rough triangles with quite thin, raggedy edges. Place them around the cone to form petals. Continue until you get the fullness you want, opening the petals as you go. Trim off the bottom of the cone just before you place it on the cake.

Calla lilies are great looking and easy to do. Pinch off an egg-sized lump of white dough and roll it out flat, about ¼ inch thick. Cut a large petal shape, about 6 or 7 inches long for a good-sized flower. Take a small piece of wax paper, crumple it into a small roll, and drape the top of the petal shape over it so it looks curved and lilylike.

Pinch off a small strip of dough, color it bright yellow, roll it into a long, thin, rounded shape and put it in the center of the petal so it looks like the stamen. Fold the lower sides of the petal over the stamen and curve the edges to look authentic. Pinch off an egg-sized lump of dough

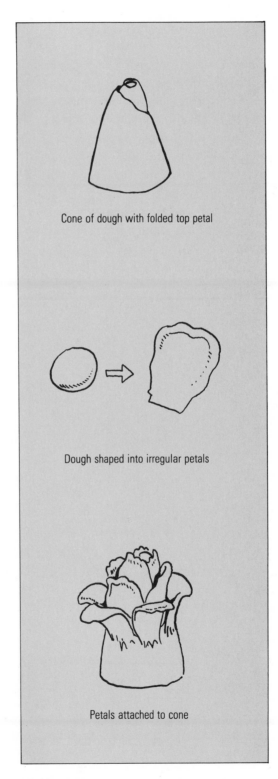

Cone of dough with folded top petal

Dough shaped into irregular petals

Petals attached to cone

Making a rose

and color it bright green for the stem and leaves. Roll a strip for the stem measuring about 2 inches high and 4 inches long and cut a wide serrated edge into the top. Put the strip, serrations up, around the base of the petal and mold it into a stem.

Take the remaining green dough, roll out a long strip, and cut long, narrow lily fronds from it. Score each leaf down the center with a knife and attach the leaves to the stem, curving them to look real. Use a bit of egg white for glue if the stem is too dry for the leaves to attach.

As you can see, the possibilities for

molding shapes are limitless. Gisella says she successfully has used flights of butterflies and/or birds made of fondant or marzipan on wedding cakes, suspending some small ones on long needles above the cake. If any decorations survive the cake cutting, they can be retrieved, frozen, and used on other baked goods. Caterers often have a stash of decorations in their freezers, ready to go on demand.

The flavored fondant or marzipan dough can also be used with cookie cutters to make good nonfloral decorations. Gisella suggests that you consider using the

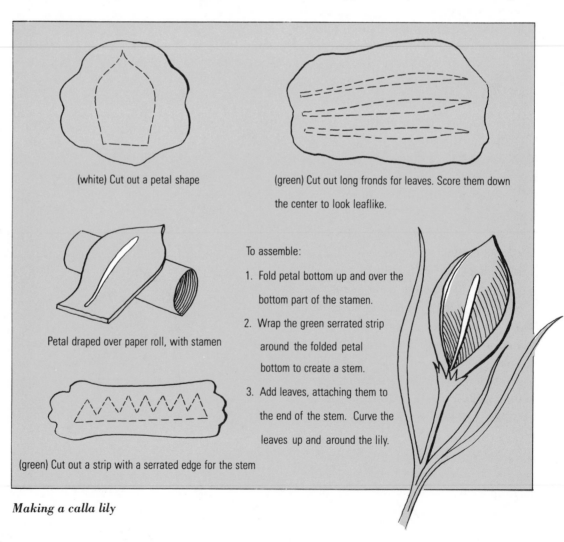

(white) Cut out a petal shape

(green) Cut out long fronds for leaves. Score them down the center to look leaflike.

Petal draped over paper roll, with stamen

(green) Cut out a strip with a serrated edge for the stem

To assemble:

1. Fold petal bottom up and over the bottom part of the stamen.

2. Wrap the green serrated strip around the folded petal bottom to create a stem.

3. Add leaves, attaching them to the end of the stem. Curve the leaves up and around the lily.

Making a calla lily

shapes for place cards, mementoes, or garnishes for dessert platters before the wedding cake is served. Simply roll out a sheet of the dough, tinted or white, and cut out shapes. Heart and bell shapes are appropriate for weddings, or cut a shape you like out of heavy cardboard and use it as a pattern, tracing around it with a sharp knife. Place the shapes on wax paper to air dry and go on to make the decoration icing.

Royal Icing is the one and only mixture that always works to write on or decorate pastry. Prepare a bowl of white icing, di-vide it into small bowls, and tint with food coloring. Royal Icing hardens rapidly, so keep it covered with a sheet of plastic placed directly on the surface so no air can get it. If it does harden, thin it with a few drops of lemon juice. Don't use water for thinning, or it will fall apart.

ROYAL ICING

1 large egg white
1½ cups confectioners' sugar

Whisk together and cover tightly!

You'll need some pastry bags with fine,

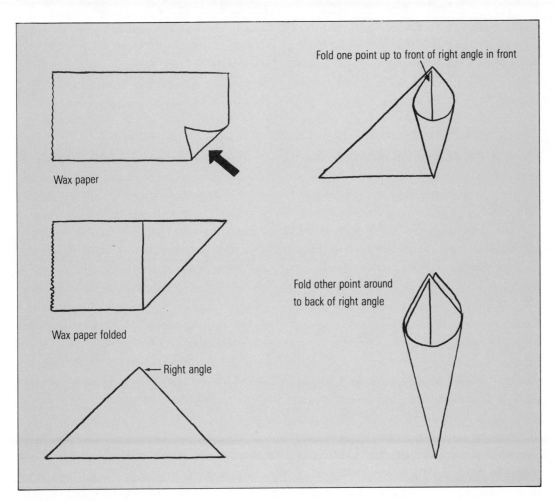

Making a pastry bag

number 1 or number 2 points, to use for writing and decorating. Gisella showed us how to make disposable pastry bags from wax paper:

On a sheet of wax paper about 18 inches long, fold one top corner diagonally down to match the side of the paper. Trim off the excess paper at the open bottom and cut through the fold on top, forming two triangles of paper. Each has a 90-degree angle and two smaller angles. Hold the paper in front of you with the 90-degree angle pointing up. Take one of the other angle points and scroll the paper in front, pulling it up so that the two points match. Hold the points together in your fingers and take the remaining angle point and scroll it around in back of the paper, pulling it up so it matches the other points you are holding.

What you have is a sturdy wax paper cone or pastry bag. Staple the points together at the top and roll the stapled part over a few times to form a firm edge. Put some icing into the bag and with a scissors, clip a tiny opening in the point. Practice squeezing the bag gently so the icing comes out in an even, thin line. Make a paper pastry bag for each color of icing you need, and you're ready to go!

A simple decoration called Cortelli Lace is easy to do and looks terrific on wedding shapes. Simply pipe a thin border of icing around each shape and then fill in the middle with fine wiggly lines of icing until it is all filled in and looks lacy. This looks best when using only one color of icing. Gisella suggests that you make many lace bells and hearts and put them all around the vertical surfaces of theweddingcake.

Once you feel easy with a pastry bag you can go on to script, writing the bride's and groom's name and perhaps the date on the dough shape or a message of your choice. It certainly opens up many possibilities!

Another good, easy use for Royal Icing and a pastry bag is on the wedding cake itself. Use it over the regular buttercream icing to create fancy effects. Gisella suggests something called "stringwork" which is time-consuming but guaranteed to dazzle. It can be done on the vertical or the horizontal surfaces. For vertical, put a small dot of icing on the cake and then gently pull the bag away, making a hanging loop of icing. Put the bag back and attach the loop a ½ inch or so away from the first dot. Continue around the cake, making fine, looped festoons of icing. You control the depth of the loop by how far away you pull the pastry bag.

Make one complete circle of loops all around the cake layer and then go back over it two more times, building up dimension by the thickness of the icing. After three times around, you're ready for the finishing touch. This time around make much shorter icing loops, just connecting the top dots with a little hanging down. The total effect is terrific, very dimensional, creating a light-and-shadow look. You don't have to restrict yourself to one set of festoons. The loops can be made all the way down the vertical surface, getting a dimensional fish scale look.

Stringwork is perfect also for the horizontal surfaces. Very lightly sketch a design into the icing on the cake, using the head of a pin or a small skewer, just enough so you can follow the pattern. You can get into very baroque, scrolly designs with lots of curlicues if you want since Royal Icing is fluid enough to follow fine details.

Pipe a thin line of icing around the pattern and go over it four or five times, building up dimension as you work. The dimensional stringwork can be used effectively in combination with other decorations; for example, you can make a pretty pattern on the cake and then tuck molded dough roses and leaves into the curves. The possibilities are endless, and it's all fun to do.

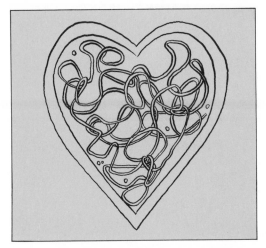 

Fondant heart with Cortelli Lace and cake decorated with fondant hearts

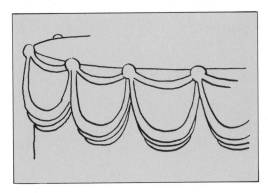 

Stringwork   *Stringwork with flowers*

▼ *The Wedding Feast worksheets can be found on pages 220–21.*

▲▲▲▲▲▲▲

15

PREPARING AND PRESENTING YOUR FEAST TO ITS BEST ADVANTAGE

▼▼▼▼▼▼▼

O nce the menu is established you can begin matching the volunteer cooks with the foods to be prepared. Make sure everybody knows that you expect to supply the ingredients; their gift to you is the preparation and the cooking. Buying the ingredients in quantity will save you money, especially if you have access to wholesale meat and produce markets.

You should supply recipes to volunteer cooks if you possibly can do so without insulting them. If, for example, you have six people each making lasagna for fifteen, each pan does not have to taste the same, but it's a good idea to have everybody know what everybody else is using. Another good idea is to send brand-new meat thermometers along with roasts you drop off at friends' houses. If "rare" is important, make sure it will happen!

Very few people have had hands-on experience with quantity cooking, but most experienced home cooks can turn out disaster-free dishes for ten to fifteen people. Attempt to keep each volunteer's amounts in keeping with his or her skills. Your wedding is no place to let someone try his hand at cooking for one hundred.

The ingredients distribution is relatively easy to organize, but the food pickup needs some attention. Find a volunteer who will drive around on the morning of the wedding to pick up the prepared foods and transport them to the reception party space. A station wagon is the ideal vehicle. Be ready to supply a plastic drop cloth and plenty of paper towels. Use the workbook page 222 to gather addresses and phone numbers and work out the routes, then photocopy it and give each volunteer a copy.

Chef Henry Archer Meer, of Lutece, graciously offered some professional cooking advice:

"For canapes, don't go overboard. They are there simply to stimulate the appetite. Think of what's still to come. Canapes are time-consuming to prepare. Do them the day before, wrap tightly with plastic wrap, and refrigerate. Use many different kinds of breads for cold canapes, and see if you can buy the loaves unsliced. Remove the crusts and thinly slice them horizontally; it will save you time and money.

"White bread should be very lightly toasted to firm it up; dark breads can be used as they come. Cut breads into fancy shapes with cookie cutters or a sharp knife. Always use a moisturizer on the bread shapes so they won't dry out or get soggy. A thin coating of butter or margarine is best; mayonnaise and mustard also work. Use a pastry bag to fill and/or decorate the bread. Research magazines and gourmet cookbooks for fillings and presentation ideas. Most important: Don't overload the canapes!

"Hot canapes need an oven, but they add a little zing to a party. Use the frozen puff paste, rolled thin, to wrap around things, to be cut into shapes and baked, or fit into very small muffin tins to make tartlet shells. Fill the shells with well spiced combinations of almost anything:

quiche filling with cheese
tomato with zuccini (ratatouille or caponata filling)
mushrooms with bacon
sausage and eggs
anchovies with tomato
crabmeat and other seafood

"For the buffet, consider pâtés and galantines and rillettes as other cold meats if you don't want to get into carving. Pâté is merely the French word for meatloaf. Everybody knows how to make meatloaf; just read a few gourmet cookbooks to get ideas for interesting combinations of meats, vegetables, nuts, and spices that will make the meatloaf into party food.

"A galantine is easy to make if you have a butcher who will bone turkeys or large chickens for you. A galantine is a boneless, stuffed bird that is rolled, tied, and poached in stock or consomme. It is served in slices. The stuffing can go in many directions, from plain bread and sausage to fancy pâtés and vegetables. Check gourmet cookbooks for recipes. A galantine can be prepared in advance, looks great, and is a sure hit alone or with a few pouring sauces.

"Rillettes are little known to Americans; however, the old school lunchbox standby, deviled ham, is a rillette. The cooking method is rather easy, and rillettes keep for weeks under refrigeration. Check cookbooks for specifics. An assortment of meats and/or poultry is boiled in animal fat, wine, and spices until the meats disintegrate. Bones are then removed, and the meat shreds are packed in crocks and sealed with some of the melted fat, which is removed right before serving. One combination I like, duck legs and pork shoulder cooked in rendered duck fat, white wine, pepper, thyme, and bay leaf, makes tasty but inexpensive party food.

"Poaching a whole fish is easy when done the professional way. Ask your fishmonger for the freshest whole salmon, bass, and so forth, and have him clean it and remove the gills. Season with salt and pepper, and put some fresh herbs such as tarragon, thyme, and bay leaf in the belly. Wrap the whole fish in cheesecloth and tie securely with string.

"Make a court bouillon cooking liquid that is one-third dry white wine and two-thirds water with a hearty splash of tarragon vinegar. Add parsley, bay leaf, tarragon, chopped onions, celery, and peppercorns. Optional additions are mushrooms, orange zest (peel), juniper berries, and hot chili pepper. Make enough liquid so the fish is totally covered.

"The cooking pot must be large enough to hold the fish laid flat; a large roasting pan will do. Heat the court bouillon to a boil on the stove, lower in the fish, turn down to simmer, and let cook about twenty-five minutes for an 8-to-10-pound fish. Remove from the heat and let the fish cool completely in the bouillon. You may, if you want, leave the fish in the bouillon for several days. Remove all vegetables by straining the liquid before you store it, covered, in the refrigerator.

"Before serving, unwrap the fish carefully. Remove the skin with a fork; it will come off easily. Serve on a garnished platter. Yes, there are bones, but people will know that when they see a whole fish and be careful. The traditional accompaniment for fish is a green sauce, salsa verde, made by combining mayonnaise with lots of minced watercress or other greens.

"Aspics and timbale molds work well for weddings. Make a clear aspic using any good cookbook recipe. Select interesting molds and prepare enough filling for each mold. Fillings can vary from mousses to simple potato, vegetable, or Waldorf salad. Anything goes as long as it has a mayonnaise dressing.

"Place one mold at a time on a bed of ice in a large kitchen pan. Pour the chilled aspic into each mold, filling it to the top. Let set for a few minutes, until a layer of aspic at least ⅛-inch thick has formed. Then pour the aspic out, using a circular motion to achieve a smooth coating. Decorate the coating with cutouts of truffles and vegetables dipped in aspic, if you wish. Refrigerate and continue coating until all molds are complete.

"Mix liquid aspic into the mayonnaise salad dressing in a general ratio of two parts mayonnaise to one part aspic. Dress the salad and carefully pack into the coated molds, trying not to disturb the original coating, then seal with more aspic up to the brim. Refrigerate overnight. Unmold and garnish right before serving. If you have never worked with gelatins and molds, practice this general recipe before the wedding."

Presentation is everything, all the professionals agree. From the basic table design to the garnishes on the individual platters, everything must be decorated so it bears no visual relationship to ordinary, everyday food.

Begin by planning how you want the buffet table(s) to look. "When Chow caters a party, people often know it just by the design of the tables," says Diane McIngvale of Dallas's Chow Catering. "We have a definite style, almost our trademark. We build up each buffet from the table base, using several levels on which to display the food platters. Nothing is ever just flat on the table. We frequently use a cornucopia shape, with wonderful goodies spilling out over several levels."

Alan Munn said multilevel buffets are always used on the cruise ships. "Flat presentation makes everything look as though it belongs in a cafeteria, not at a party." The flat presentation is enough of a no-no that even the platters placed right on the table are slanted and have their inner sides raised a bit, carrying the eye to the next higher level. Alan uses flat metal boxes made for this purpose. The boxes are stored in the ship's freezers until setup time, then wrapped in napkins and the platters placed on them. The boxes help keep the food chilled.

"To make home versions of these," Alan suggested, "use the home freezer chill packs wrapped in napkins. Just be sure to tuck another, folded napkin under the far edge so the platter will not sit flat."

The champagne fountain is another cruise ship favorite that can be duplicated at home with rented equipment and a little practice. Beverage and restaurant supply places usually have small pumps to rent, complete with tubing and a fake champagne bottle that the liquid pours from on top of the glasses.

"Use a large roasting pan or other deep container that will hold water. Cover it with a sheet of heavy screening, sturdy enough so it won't sag in the middle. Cover the screening with a layer of foil and punch many pinholes in the foil, small enough so they won't be visible, and a sufficient number so all the liquid falls into the pan to allow the pump to bring it back up into the fake bottle.

"Build a pyramid of champagne glasses on the screen. You can begin with thirty-two glasses, then sixteen, then eight, four, and two, or any combination that will give you a pyramid effect. Definitely use plastic champagne glasses for your first few attempts to set up the fountain. It's a bit tricky to balance when you first turn the pump on. I must have gone through two dozen actual champagne glasses the first time I tried it, before I thought of plastic.

"Never use real champagne in the

Champagne fountain

PREPARING AND PRESENTING YOUR FEAST

fountain. The bubbles get worked out in the first five minutes so it's a waste. Use generic ginger ale or tint tap water to look like champagne or wine."

Another cruise ship presentation Alan discussed was the use of ice carvings as a buffet focal point. Ice, lighted either from below or above, becomes a sparkly, diamondlike object that's hard to beat. It takes a real professional to come up with a good looking ice carving, but a perfect substitute for the do-it-yourself wedding is the ice mold, which restaurant supply stores generally carry. The molds, complete with directions, come in many shapes and cost between ten and thirty dollars. They are two-piece molds that you fit together, fill with water, and freeze. Alan suggests tinting the water a pastel version of one of your wedding colors for extra pizzazz.

Take the mold to the table in a large, foil-lined pan and then camouflage it with some of your table decorations. The larger the mold, the longer it will last, says Alan. Put out the mold minutes before the guests walk in. A medium-sized mold will last for about two and a half or three hours and then should be removed. Be sure to have a flower arrangement ready to replace it so your buffet table doesn't look tacky for the rest of the party.

Henry Meer's buffets at Lutece are also multileveled. A main focal point is designed first, perhaps a floral arrangement, a fruit basket, or an ice carving. It is placed highest and is lighted with a tiny spotlight. Two or three other platters are elevated, each on a separate level, all below the level of the focal point display. The guest's eyes are drawn to the focal point and then move down from level to

Multilevel buffet

Weighted box covered in fabric

level to the tabletop. The whole display is lovely and looks nothing like home!

Use open wooden boxes or heavy cardboard containers of different sizes and shapes to form your levels. Cover each box with a tableclothlike fabric that can't be seen through. Tape or staple the cloths around the boxes and place them over something heavy, such as a stack of books, so they are not easily moved. Henry cautions: "Make sure your buffet table elevations are well built and sturdy. Remember, people will be picking and pushing at them."

Use serving platters of many different shapes, sizes, and materials. "We never do anything all on silver," Diane offers. "It doesn't have to be silver to make it nice. Our most spectacular parties have been when we used no silver at all. We have used a mix of black lacquer trays,

baskets spray painted white, and glass, mirror, or Lucite."

Henry described a student exercise in platter design from his alma mater, the Culinary Institute of America in Hyde Park, New York. Foods are not to touch the frame of any tray or platter. The space between food elements is very important; foods should never be crowded onto a tray.

Most buffet platters have three design elements:

1) the main item (centerpiece), which is displayed whole, minus slices that have been pre-cut;

2) the slices, artistically arranged;

3) the garnish, in good proportion to the centerpiece.

Rectangular, round, and oval trays are divided into six or eight sections:

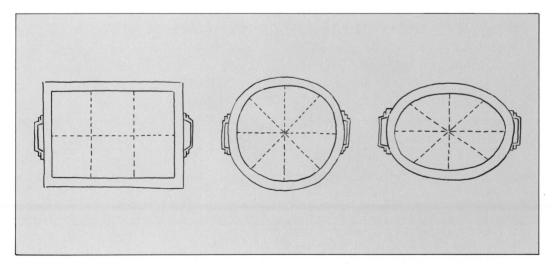

Divided platters

PREPARING AND PRESENTING YOUR FEAST

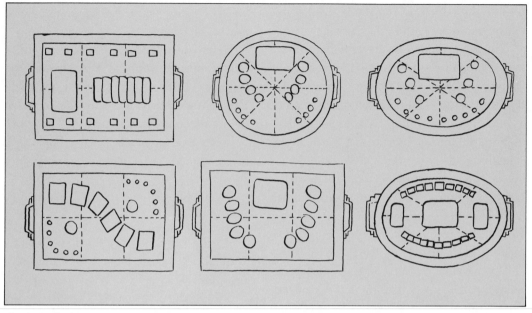

Arranged platters

The three elements are arranged on each tray using the grid for easy accuracy. Some classic placements are shown above.

Select some of these placements or create your own; post them in the party space kitchen as reference material when you are setting up the platters before the reception begins. By settling on the platter designs in advance you'll speed up the on-site work and will be able to make the right kind and number of garnishes beforehand. Then, as the service commences, your kitchen manager can be sure each platter is perfect before it makes its debut on the buffet table.

"Never put all the food on the buffet at once," Diane says. "We always prepare two trays of each item, one to serve and one for backup. Once a platter has been served from, it's no longer pretty. Each time somebody else takes some food, the platter gets more and more messy.

"Our buffet manager keeps a close watch on the condition of the platters and replaces a messy platter with its duplicate before it really gets terrible looking. Then the kitchen manager can repair the original platter, add food to it, and have it ready to reappear when the duplicate needs to be redone. Part of Chow's reputation depends on having the tables look terrific, so we're very particular.

"If there are many guests, we'll do a 'mirror buffet' to speed up the service. The buffet is spread over a very long table, with duplicate platters on each side of a major centerpiece. The serving plates and flatware are in the middle. Guests line up in the center, take their plates, and then turn to the right or the left for the food. For mirror buffets we prepare two duplicate platters, one for each side, and two more for backups."

Alan Munn says he tries to avoid mirror buffets because they tend to confuse the guests. Nobody seems sure that both lines are getting the identical foods, so people tend to wander around, checking things out and getting in the way. "We know that one hundred and fifty people can go through a one-sided buffet line in about thirty to forty-five minutes, and we can speed that up a bit by using servers."

Alan adds, "You have more flexibility at a wedding than on a ship. The best man can do some crowd control by calling tables up two or three at a time once the bridal party has gotten their food. Still, once you get near three hundred guests, a mirror buffet is certainly a possibility."

"One big point I always have to go over with every new staff has nothing to do with food service but is vital: Always make sure the legs on all the tables are locked in place and that the legs of tables used together are tied or wired to each other. Buffet tables get much more jostling and pushing than you'd ever believe, so make sure your party doesn't end up on the floor!"

Once you have worked out some platter designs you need to think about garnishes. There are many excellent reference books in libraries and bookstores. Japanese and Chinese cuisines take garnishing to sublime heights, and several exciting paperbound books are available to furnish you with instructions.

Food needs to be displayed on a base before any of the fancy, carved garnishes are added. "Mother Nature has provided us with great backdrops for platters in the many types of greenery available in most markets," says Henry. "Think about curly chicory, watercress, iceberg, lamb's, red leaf, romaine, and Boston lettuce, radicchio, spinach and, the old standby, parsley. Be sure to wash all greens thoroughly in several waters to remove the sand before arranging on platters."

If you have unlimited access to fresh flowers, use them as garnishes on platters. Keep a large vase in the kitchen and tuck blossoms around the food, on top of the greenery base. Fresh flowers will save you a lot of time making garnishes, and the presentation will be festive.

Although not used onboard a cruise ship, Alan gave us directions for a flower garnish he produced for his own wedding. Daisies, his wife's favorite flower, were the wedding bouquet. He decided to extend the theme into the garnishes by embedding daisies into clear aspic and using them on canape and food platters.

Use powdered gelatin from the supermarket and mix a large proportion of gelatin to water, so the mixture will gel very stiff. Pour about ½ inch into flat pans and let it get firm. Once it's firm to the touch,

Using fresh flowers as garnishes makes a festive presentation and saves time

PREPARING AND PRESENTING YOUR FEAST

place the flowers, blossoms only, on the gelatin and carefully pour more gelatin into the pan to cover the flowers fully. Chill until everything has hardened, then cut around each flower but do not remove from the pan. Just before serving, lift out each flower with a spatula and put it into place on a platter. (Alan said the daisies looked as though they were embedded in sparkly Lucite, and this unassuming flower made rather important looking decorations.

Another gelatin use, this one from the cruise ships, is to color tap water with vegetable coloring, mix it with powdered gelatin, and let it harden until very stiff. When fully firm, chop it up into small, sparkly pieces and use them as the base for meat platters. The colored gelatin may be used alone or placed over a border of leaves or ferns. Alan recommends this especially for rather pale meats such as turkey or chicken roll. Nobody really eats the gelatin, but nobody will get sick if a bit clings to a meat slice!

Henry Meer has furnished us with directions to make a number of his favorite vegetable garnishes. "All you need," says Henry, "is a very sharp paring knife, a vegetable peeler, toothpicks, and a large bowl of ice water. And time. Practice these beforehand. You can actually carve most of them the day before the wedding. Store overnight in ice water, integrate them into your platter designs, and you're all set."

There are many vegetable garnishes that look like flowers. Use them in combination with real leaves, ferns, or parsley to further the floral look:

Scallion and Leek Thistle: Trim green tops and lower roots from the vegetable.

Make a series of cuts very close together all the way around the white part, taking care to leave ½ inch of the bottom uncut. Place in a bowl of ice water; the cold will make the cut strips puff out and become flowerlike. The vegetables can be tinted to match your wedding colors by adding a few drops of food coloring to the water. Make the day before and store overnight in cold water.

A variation can be done on the leeks. Space the cuts about ¼ inch apart rather than very close together. Beginning with the outer layer, tuck the cut ends back into the base of the leek. Continue almost to the top, leaving a few center fronds standing up as a center for the flower. Tint with food coloring if you like.

Onion, Radish, and Beet Pom Poms: Choose rather evenly formed firm vegetables. Peel the onions and the beets; scrub the radishes. Cut off the stems and roots, leaving a flat base. Make a series of cuts through the vegetables, leaving ½ inch to ¼ inch of the base uncut. Turn the vegetables 90 degrees and make identical cuts. Put the radishes and the beets in ice water until the cut parts puff open. Place the onions in a bowl of hot water first and leave them for five or ten minutes to remove the strong odor, then put them into the ice water to puff up. Tint the onions with food coloring in the ice water or by brushing diluted color onto the tips and centers of the "flowers."

Radish Rose: Trim the roots and stems off well scrubbed radishes. Make a series of cuts around the outside, forming petals that are red on the outside and white within. Continue cutting, leaving a small center in each. Store in ice water to puff up.

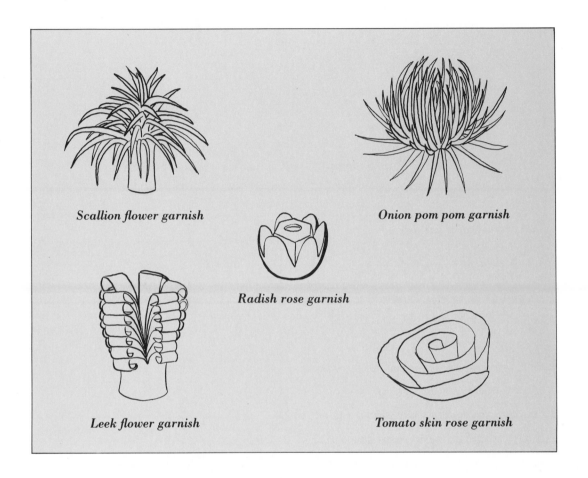

Scallion flower garnish

Onion pom pom garnish

Radish rose garnish

Leek flower garnish

Tomato skin rose garnish

Tomato Skin Roses: Use medium or large tomatoes. With a paring knife cut long strips of skin, as thin as possible, about 1 inch high and 4 inches long. Beginning at one end, coil a strip tightly to form the inner blossom. Add another strip, making looser coils to form the outer petals. Place carefully on platters. Tomato roses cannot be made in advance but take so little time to cut they can be done just before serving.

Beet Skin Roses: Similar to tomato skin roses except they can be done in advance. Trim off roots and stems and peel the beets. Cut long strips of beet as thin as possible, about 1 inch high and 4 inches long. Soak in ice water to soften and make

flexible. Coil the same as tomato skin rose.

Carrot Flowers: These are small, four-petal blossoms cut from the tip of a "sharpened" carrot. Peel each carrot. Make four thin cuts diagonally downward, almost through the carrot, to form the four equal petals. Gently twist the cut portion, and it will pop off and look like a little flower. Store in ice water. Scatter these in groups around the greens on a platter for small spots of color.

Apple Bird: For a "knock 'em dead" garnish it's hard to beat the apple bird. Begin with a large Delicious apple. Cut a slice off one side so it sits firmly. Reserve the cut slice to make the head and neck.

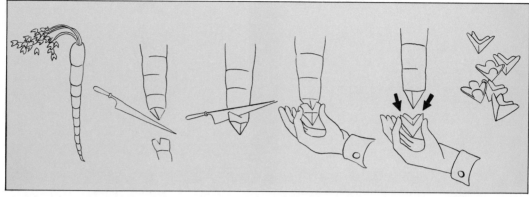

Small carrot flower garnish

Apple bird garnish

1. Cut a slice off the bottom of the apple.

2. Carve a neck, with head and beak, out of the apple slice. Leave apple skin on. Reserve cut piece.

3. Set apple on sliced side and cut two large pieces out, leaving an uncut strip on the center top.

4. Carve layers from the cut-out pieces, following the shape of the apple and making sure the apple skin is intact on each layer. Cut as many layers as possible from each piece.

5. To assemble: Cut a groove into the apple (the apple bird's body) opposite where the apple stem would be. Shape the groove to the size of the base of the neck-and-head piece. Attach the head-and-neck section into the groove of the apple with a toothpick, then put the cut pieces back into the apple and fan the slices back to form the wings.

6. Spray the bird with water and lemon juice to stop it from browning, and refrigerate until needed.

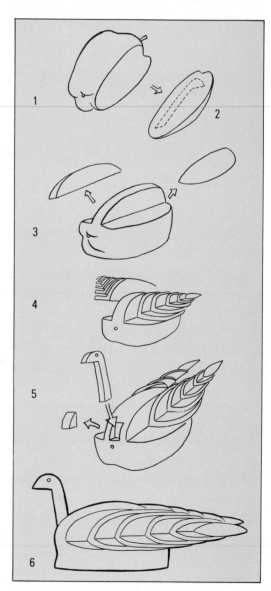

Mark a horizontal band about ¼ inch wide on the top of the apple. Cut a wide triangle of apple out of each side, using the edges of the band as the cutting guide. Reserve the apple while you cut a series of very thin "V" shapes from the triangles, cutting until all the apple is used.

Fan out the triangles, overlapping them, and place them back into the spaces they were cut from, forming wings that extend beyond the end of the apple. Cut a neck and head shape out of the piece you sliced off the bottom. Attach the neck and head pieces to the front of the apple with a toothpick.

Store the entire bird submerged in water to which lemon juice has been added. Assemble just before serving and squeeze lemon juice over it to keep it from turning brown.

Sweet dishes also need to be garnished. Two easy, make-ahead decorations are the following:

Frosted Grapes: Cut small bunches of firm, well formed grapes. Dip into beaten egg white that has been diluted with a little cold water, then sprinkle or dip the clusters into sugar, either powdered or granulated, to get a frosted effect. Use cinnamon sugar or cake decorating sprinkles for a more colorful effect. If you are sure nobody will eat them, sprinkle glitter on the grapes.

Chocolate Leaves: This unbelievably simple garnish looks fabulous on any dessert. Pick, wash, and dry sturdy leaves from any household or garden greenery; ivy, philodendron, and ficus tree leaves all work well. Avoid leaves that have fuzz or "hair" on them.

Melt an ounce or two of chocolate bits or a chocolate bar in a double boiler. When the chocolate is liquid, paint a medium thick coating of chocolate on the undersides of the leaves using a small paintbrush or pastry brush. Don't get any chocolate on the edges or top of each leaf. Lay the leaves on a plate and refrigerate until the chocolate is firm. Before serving, carefully peel off the chocolate, beginning with the stem end. It will come off easily. Use these chocolate leaves on mousses, cold soufflés, cake, and so forth.

Cups and boats can be made from vegetable and fruits and are a fun way to serve small condiments or individual portions of anything:

Orange, Lemon, or Grapefruit Cups: Cut fruits in half. Run a serrated grapefruit knife around the pulp and scrape it out with a spoon. Wrap in plastic and refrigerate until needed. Fill and garnish before serving.

The edges of the cups can be cut in a decorative zigzag pattern. Cups can be made into baskets by marking a band ¼ inch wide across the top of the fruit. Cut out two triangles and carefully scrape out the fruit, leaving a peel basket with handle.

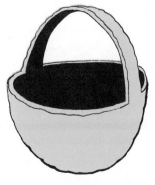

An orange, lemon, or grapefruit cup

PREPARING AND PRESENTING YOUR FEAST

Tomato and Pepper Cups: Cut off one-third of the vegetables from the stem end. Remove pulp and seeds to form cups. Edges can be cut decoratively if you want. If necessary, cut a thin slice off the ends so the vegetables stand upright. Store the peppers in ice water; salt the tomatoes and refrigerate, wrapped in plastic, until needed.

Cucumber and Zucchini Boats: Trim a thin slice off the bottom of the vegetables to make them sit flat. Cut off the upper one-third of the vegetables, cutting from end to end. The edges may be cut decoratively. Using a melon baller, carefully scoop out the insides. Refrigerate, wrapped in plastic, until needed.

Cabbage Bowl: Select good looking red or green cabbage and remove any tired looking outer leaves. Cut a thin slice off the bottom so it stands firmly and cut off one-third of the top. Cut and remove the inner leaves until you have a bowl. Fill with dip or sauce; use the top for a cover.

• • •

For large serving containers nothing beats carved melons. The approach to carving them is a bit different from carving vegetables since you need to make a paper pattern, trace it onto the melon, and then cut on the pattern lines. There are almost no limits to what sort of container you can make: boats, baskets, urns, punch bowls, swans, whales, baby carriages, and so on. Here's an old favorite, Moby Dick:

Watermelon Whale: Choose an evenly colored melon and trim a thin slice off the bottom so it sits firmly. The stem end will be the whale's face, the other end the tail.

Turn the melon so you are facing the stem end and trace a horizontal arching curve to delineate the face. Extend the face lines backward and begin to curve them upward for the tail.

Take a small piece of newspaper, fold it in half, and draw half a whale's tail, beginning with the folded edge. Cut out the tail half, open the paper, and place the tail on the melon. Keep clipping and trying tails until you get one that is sufficiently jaunty and in good scale with your melon. Trace it on the melon, connecting with the extended face lines.

Cut a 2-inch X on the top of the melon to relieve the pressure and begin to cut along the traced lines. Work in small sections, removing pieces as you cut. Remove the pulp and use it in fruit salad, and so forth. Cut or scratch facial features on the stem end; poke a stalk of baby's breath into the top of the face for a blow-hole.

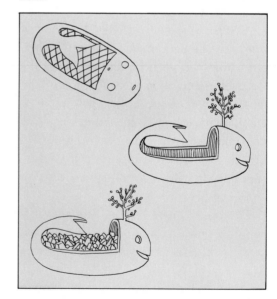

Watermelon whale

▼ *The Wedding Feast worksheets can be found on pages 220–21.*

▲▲▲▲▲▲▲

EPILOGUE

▼▼▼▼▼▼▼

16

As to Catherine and Greg's wedding, everyone agrees that it was a smashing success. Guests who attended but did not work on it were amazed to hear that it was a homegrown effort. We, the corps de volontaires, were equally amazed that we had gotten it all together. It really worked!

We had worked very hard—longer hours and greater effort than anybody had anticipated. "But," as someone concluded, "the trouble with doing it yourself is that you really have to do it." I think, in retrospect, combining the do-it-yourself aspect with some hired professionals would have made life easier. We spread ourselves a bit thin; on the other hand, we did manage to stay within our rather minimal budget.

My favorite memories center on the differences of expectation between Greg's family and ours. It seemed to be a "traditional catered affair" approach versus a "Hey guys! let's put on a terrific wedding" approach.

Although everybody enjoyed the wedding, some members of Greg's family still describe it as "very different." And to the end of her days, Greg's grandmother referred to the unorthodox but beautifully designed handmade invitations as "those fliers you sent out for your wedding."

The wedding feast caused concern in both clans. They were worried that we would not serve enough food and that that would be embarrassing. We were worried because it all had to look enchanting and taste marvelous. As the great day drew nearer the anxiety mounted. Secretly, after the wedding rehearsal, Greg's brother gallantly offered to send in three hundred hot hors d'oeuvres if it would help. And the morning of the wedding Hank was hurriedly teaching me and two close friends how to carve garnishes like Lutece's to jazz up the food platters. Everybody acted perfectly loony, and it all turned out well. The buffet was a beaut, and there were lots of leftovers.

One positive aftereffect was the sure feeling that I/we can put on an excellent, smoothly functioning, large party for any occasion. Be it a christening, a wake, or a Happy Halloween bash, the understructure of a big party remains the same. Once you've learned how to do it, you can repeat all or any parts as often as you want.

The thing I liked best about the wedding, aside from acquiring a good friend/ son-in-law, was the sense of community we all felt. Since then we have worked on other friends' weddings and have truly basked in the good feelings. Teamwork brings many of its own rewards.

A month or so after Catherine and Greg's marriage many of the Carlottis attended an elegant catered wedding on a cruise ship. I was standing with Gino, the dear friend who had done an incredible job organizing and running our bar and beverage service. I wanted to move a chair, so I asked him to help. He grinned and said, "No, no. I'm not working this wedding."

EPILOGUE

▲▲▲▲▲▲▲

WEDDING
WORKSHEETS

▼▼▼▼▼▼▼

17

CONCEPT

I imagine my ideal wedding to look like:

Bride_____   Groom_____

_____   _____

_____   _____

_____   _____

A composite ideal wedding for both of us is_____

_____

_____

_____

_____

Four of my favorite places and what I like about each:

Bride_____   Groom_____

_____   _____

_____   _____

_____   _____

Three words that describe the feeling of each place:

Bride_____   Groom_____

_____   _____

_____   _____

_____   _____

We want our wedding place to feel like_____

_____

_____

_____

My favorite colors are:

Bride_____   Groom_____

_____   _____

In my ideal wedding I am wearing:

Bride_____   Groom_____

_____   _____

_____   _____

Our wedding colors will be_____

_____

Flowers we want to include in our wedding:_____

_____

Flowers that will be in season for our wedding:_____

_____

Special effects I would like to include in our wedding:

Bride_____   Groom_____

_____   _____

_____   _____

▲▲▲▲▲▲▲

CALENDAR

▼▼▼▼▼▼▼

Wedding date_____ Time_____

Parents' Meeting(s)

Date_____ Place_____' Time_____

_____ _____ _____

Wedding party selected_____

_____

_____

Budgets established

	Date	Amount
Ceremony space		
Reception space		
Invitations and announcements		
Costumes		
Flowers		
Sound		
Lighting		
Decor and props		
Beverages		
Photography		
Food		
Transportation		
Miscellaneous		
	TOTAL:	

Ceremony location selected (date)_____ Deposit paid_____

Reception location selected (date) _____Deposit paid_____

Wedding trip planned_____Reservations made_____

Photography appointments: Engagement photo_____Wedding photo_____

Engagement announcement to be mailed_____

Wedding announcement to be mailed_____

Invitations completed by (date)_____   Date to be mailed_____

Clothing selected by_____   Final fitting dates_____

_____

_____

Flowers selected (date)_____   Date to be ordered_____

Sound and music to be   Advance planning and

selected (date)_____   work dates_____

_____

Lighting to be designed (date)_____   Advance planning and work dates_____

_____

Beverage menu to be selected (date)____   Date to order_____

Menu established (date)_____   Advance planning and work dates_____

_____   _____

Bridesmaids' luncheon

date_____   Location_____   Given by_____

Wedding shower(s)

date_____   Location_____   Given by_____

_____   _____   _____

_____   _____   _____

_____   _____   _____

Bachelor party date_____   Location_____   Given by_____

Medical exam and blood tests   Location_____

date_____

Marriage license to be gotten by_____

Wedding rehearsal date_____   Time_____

Rehearsal dinner location_____   Time_____

Time schedule for wedding day:

Ceremony begins_____   Dancing begins_____

Reception begins_____   Wedding cake presentation_____

Receiving line begins_____   Bridal couple leave reception_____

Cocktail service begins_____   Reception ends_____

Food service begins_____

CEREMONY CHECKLIST

Church or temple address _____

_____

Phone _____

Contact _____

Seating capacity of the sanctuary _____

Other events at church or temple scheduled for your day _____

_____

Costs—amount and date to be paid:

Fee for use of building _____

Fee for clergyman _____

Organist _____

Choir _____

Parking facilities _____

Fee for traffic and parking attendants _____

Additional people participating in traditional service: _____

Person:	Contribution:
_____	_____
_____	_____
_____	_____

Special rules about:

Photography _____

Videotaping _____

Flowers _____

Candles _____

Bride's carpet _____

Aisle ribbons _____

Flower girl strewing real petals down the aisle_____

_____

Use of rice, confetti, birdseed to shower the newlyweds_____

_____

Printed wedding service programs_____

Music:
Meeting with music director_____
Incidental music_____
Processional_____
Favorite selections_____

_____

Recessional_____

_____

Equipment rentals_____

_____

_____

Time schedule:
Wedding rehearsal_____
Day of wedding_____

_____

_____

_____

CHRISTIAN PROCESSIONAL

▼▼▼▼▼▼▼

WEDDING WORKSHEETS

Name	Address and Phone	Sizes
Bride		
Father of Bride		
Flower Girl		
Ring Bearer		
Maid of Honor		
Matron of Honor		
Bridesmaid		
Bridesmaid		
Bridesmaid		
Bridesmaid		
Bridesmaid		
Bridesmaid		
Head Usher		
Usher		
Usher		
Usher		
Usher		
Usher		
Groom		
Best Man		
Clergyman		

▲▲▲▲▲▲▲

CHRISTIAN RECESSIONAL

▼▼▼▼▼▼▼

Bride and Groom

Flower Girl

Ring Bearer

Maid of Honor
and
Best Man

Matron of Honor
and
Head Usher

Bridesmaids
and
Ushers

Clergyman

WEDDING WORKSHEETS

▲▲▲▲▲▲▲

TRADITIONAL JEWISH PROCESSIONAL

▼▼▼▼▼▼▼

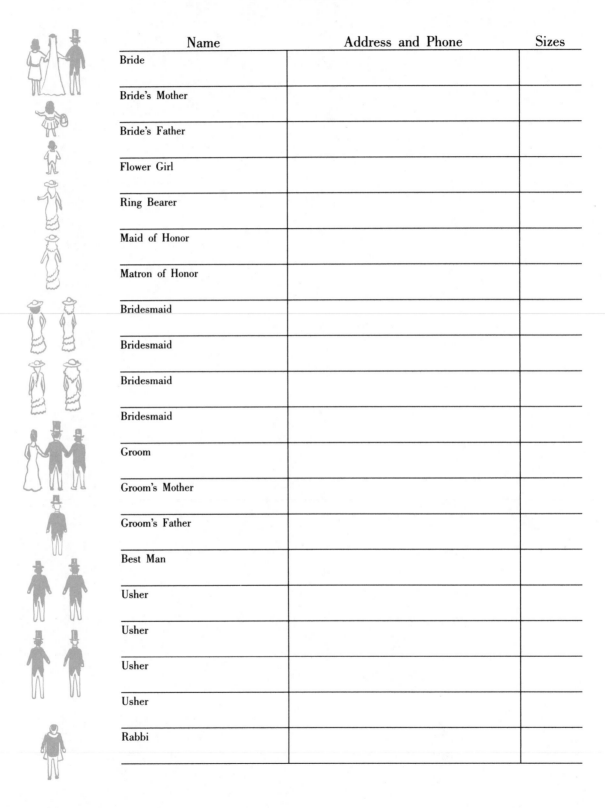

Name	Address and Phone	Sizes
Bride		
Bride's Mother		
Bride's Father		
Flower Girl		
Ring Bearer		
Maid of Honor		
Matron of Honor		
Bridesmaid		
Bridesmaid		
Bridesmaid		
Bridesmaid		
Groom		
Groom's Mother		
Groom's Father		
Best Man		
Usher		
Usher		
Usher		
Usher		
Rabbi		

TRADITIONAL JEWISH RECESSIONAL

Bride and Groom

Flower Girl

Ring Bearer

Bride's Parents

Groom's Parents

Maid of Honor
and
Best Man

Matron of Honor
and
Head Usher

Bridesmaids
and
Ushers

Rabbi

LOCATION

WEDDING WORKSHEETS

TOTAL BUDGET:_____

	Ceremony	Reception
Location	_____	_____
Contact	_____	_____
Phone	_____	_____

Costs:	Ceremony	Reception
Heat	_____	_____
Electricity	_____	_____
Insurance	_____	_____
Security	_____	_____
Security	_____	_____
Cleanup	_____	_____
Other	_____	_____

Ceremony Total_____   Reception Total_____

TOTAL LOCATION COSTS_____

Deposit amount_____   Deposit amount_____
Date_____   Date_____
Check #_____   Check #_____

COPY PAGES FOR ANNOUNCEMENTS

Engagement Announcement

Rough draft:_____

_____

_____

_____

_____

_____

_____

_____

_____

_____

_____

_____

Final version:_____

_____

_____

_____

_____

_____

_____

_____

_____

_____

_____

_____

WEDDING WORKSHEETS

Wedding Announcement

Rough draft:_____

_____

_____

_____

_____

_____

_____

_____

_____

_____

_____

Final version:_____

_____

_____

_____

_____

_____

_____

_____

_____

_____

_____

_____

_____

_____

_____

▲▲▲▲▲▲▲

INVITATIONS

▼▼▼▼▼▼▼

TOTAL BUDGET_____

Numbers needed: Mailing dates:

Ceremony invitations_____   Invitations_____

Reception invitations_____   Announcements_____

Reply cards_____

Announcements_____

Postage cost_____

Paper cost_____

Envelope cost_____

Artwork cost_____

Transfer type cost_____

Reproduction cost_____

Other_____

                              TOTAL COST_____

Volunteer in Charge_____   Phone_____

Reproduction done at_____

Contact_____   Phone_____

WEDDING WORKSHEETS

Wedding Invitation

Rough draft: _____

_____

_____

_____

_____

_____

_____

_____

_____

_____

_____

_____

_____

_____

Final version: _____

_____

_____

_____

_____

_____

_____

_____

_____

_____

_____

_____

_____

_____

COSTUMES

▼▼▼▼▼▼▼

TOTAL BUDGET_____

Cost

Wedding gown_____Hats and accessories_____   _____

Maid of Honor_____   _____

Matron of Honor_____   _____

Bridesmaids_____   _____

_____   _____

_____   _____

_____   _____

Flower Girl_____   _____

Ring Bearer_____   _____

Groom_____   _____

Best Man_____   _____

Ushers_____   _____

_____   _____

_____   _____

_____   _____

Bride's Mother_____   _____

Bride's Father_____   _____

Groom's Mother_____   _____

Groom's Father_____   _____

TOTAL COST_____

Volunteer in Charge_____ Phone_____

Rentals from_____Deposit_____

    Contact_____Phone_____

    Delivery date_____Return date_____

Fitting dates_____ _____ _____

Suppliers:

Bridal gown_____ Phone_____ Contact_____

Attendants_____ Phone_____ Contact_____

_____

_____

_____

_____

Shoes_____ Phone_____ Contact_____

_____ Phone_____ Contact_____

Headwear_____ Phone_____ Contact_____

Groom_____ Phone_____ Contact_____

Groomsmen_____ Phone_____ Contact_____

_____

_____

FLOWERS

WEDDING WORKSHEETS

TOTAL BUDGET_____

Flowers selected_____

_____

_____

Cost

Bride's bouquet_____   _____

Attendant's bouquets for:_____   _____

_____   _____

_____   _____

_____   _____

Flower Girl's basket_____   _____

Mothers' flowers_____   _____

_____   _____

Boutonnieres for:_____   _____

_____   _____

_____   _____

_____   _____

_____   _____

Altar flowers_____   _____

Table decorations: number of tables_____   _____

Buffet flowers_____   _____

Miscellaneous flowers_____   _____

TOTAL COST_____

Volunteer in Charge_____   Phone_____

Supplies needed_____

_____

_____

_____

_____

Materials ordered from_____

_____ Phone_____

_____ Phone_____

_____ Phone_____

Delivery date_____ Time_____

_____ _____

Tools needed_____

_____

_____

_____

SOUND

TOTAL BUDGET_____

Cost

Sound system_____ _____

_____ _____

_____ _____

_____ _____

_____ _____

_____ _____

_____ _____

Records_____ _____

_____ _____

_____ _____

Tapes_____ _____

_____ _____

_____ _____

Musicians_____

_____

Deposit_____Total fee_____

DJ_____

Deposit_____Total fee_____

TOTAL COST_____

Volunteer in Charge_____   Phone_____

Announcer_____ Phone _____

Musician contact_____ _____

Rentals_____ Contact_____ Phone_____

_____ _____ _____

_____ _____ _____

Delivery_____ Contact_____ Phone_____

_____ _____ _____

Return_____ Contact_____ Phone_____

_____ _____ _____

▲▲▲▲▲▲▲

LIGHTING

▼▼▼▼▼▼▼

TOTAL BUDGET_____

Overall lighting design_____

_____

General illumination_____

Cost

Lamp coverings_____ _____

Gels_____ _____

Japanese lanterns_____ _____

Special effects lighting_____ _____

_____ _____

Mirrored ball and rain lights_____ _____

Fairy lights_____ _____

Top hat spots_____ _____

Tulle_____ _____

Extension cords_____ _____

Track lights_____ _____

Candle lighting_____ _____

Votive candles_____ _____

Tapers_____ _____

TOTAL COST_____

Volunteer in Charge_____ Phone_____

Supplier	Contact	Phone
_____	_____	_____
_____	_____	_____

Rentals	Contact	Phone
_____	_____	_____
_____	_____	_____

Delivery of	To	Time
_____	_____	_____
_____	_____	_____

Return of	To	Time
_____	_____	_____
_____	_____	_____

▲▲▲▲▲▲▲

DECOR AND PROPS

▼▼▼▼▼▼▼

TOTAL BUDGET_____

Ceremony:	Cost
Aisle ribbons_____	_____
_____	_____
Bride's carpet_____	_____
_____	_____
Chupah_____	_____
_____	_____

Reception:	Item:	
Ceiling_____		_____
_____		_____
Walls_____		_____
_____		_____
Doors_____		_____
_____		_____
Windows_____		_____
_____		_____
Focal points_____		_____

WEDDING WORKSHEETS

Props:

Ring Bearer's pillow_____ _____

Cake knife_____ _____

Garter_____ _____

Cardboard cake_____ _____

TOTAL COST_____

Volunteer in Charge_____ Phone_____

WEDDING WORKSHEETS

BEVERAGE SERVICE

WEDDING WORKSHEETS

TOTAL BUDGET_____

Drinks menu_____

_____

	Cost
Hard liquor_____	_____
_____	_____
_____	_____
Wines_____	_____
Beer_____	_____
Sodas_____	_____
Mixers/Juices_____	_____
Punch_____	_____
Champagne_____	_____
Garnishes_____	_____
Ice_____	_____
Bar equipment_____	_____
Serving trays_____	_____
Styrofoam coolers_____	_____
Garbage cans_____	_____
Napkins and swizzle sticks_____	_____

TOTAL COST_____

Volunteer in Charge_____   Phone_____